Assessment of Chinese Military Modernisation and Its Implications for India

We want infinite energy, infinite zeal, infinite courage and infinite patience and then only will great things be achieved.

—Swami Vivekananda

Assessment of Chinese Military Modernisation and Its Implications for India

Major General P K Chakraborty (Retd)

Vivekananda International Foundation
New Delhi

PENTAGON PRESS LLP

Assessment of Chinese Military Modernisation and Its Implications for India
Major General P K Chakraborty (Retd)

ISBN 978-93-86618-91-7

First Published in 2019

Published by
PENTAGON PRESS LLP
206, Peacock Lane, Shahpur Jat
New Delhi-110049
Phones: 011-64706243, 26491568
Telefax: 011-26490600
email: rajan@pentagonpress.in
website: www.pentagonpress.in

Printed at Aegean Offset Printers, Greater Noida, U.P.

Contents

Foreword

The Vivekananda International Foundation is happy to present Major General (Retd) PK Chakravorty's book *Assessment of Chinese Military Modernisation and its Implications for India* to the public. Major General Chakravorty is a retired officer of the Indian Army. He is a student of India's national security and has studied China for many years.

In the last few years, the modernisation of China's People Liberation Army (PLA) and its defence industry have been studied extensively across the world. The modernisation of PLA is happening in the broader context of the rise of China, the erosion of liberal international order, and the Chinese challenge to the US hegemony. Most western studies focus on the implications of PLA modernisation from the perspective of China's rise and its implications for US security alliances.

What happens in China cannot but impact India. It has an unsettled boundary dispute with China. The two countries had a 72-day long military standoff in Doklam in 2017. The China-Pakistan Economic Corridor (CPEC) passes through Pakistan occupied Kashmir (PoK). The nexus between China and Pakistan is growing. China has upgraded its military infrastructure in Tibet. In this backdrop, what are the implications of PLA modernisation for India? How should India deal with assertive China, backed by a strong modern military? The author provides some answers in this book. It is our hope that the book will be received well by the readers.

New Delhi
23 May 2019

Dr Arvind Gupta
Director
VIF

*

Preface

China has remained a subject of interest ever since I joined the Indian Army. My first posting was in Assam and our operational area was in the Kameng sub division. Thereafter I commanded a unit in Arunachal with one of my sub units on the border with China. After my command I was posted to Vietnam as the Defence Attaché with accreditation to Laos and Cambodia in 1996. I was fortunate to have frequent interactions with the Chinese Defence Attachés in these countries. The first Gulf War was over and the Chinese People's Liberation Army (PLA) had commenced their military modernisation. It was during this period that Deng Xiaoping, the builder of modern Peoples Republic of China (PRC), passed away on 19 February 1997. The PLA was modernising at top speed and was confident after its precise practice missile shots close to Taiwan in 1996. The Chinese were also occupying the Spratly Islands on the South China Sea. Having observed these issues closely, I thought of researching on these changes closely and then writing a book. I kept gathering facts and kept watching the PLA modernise under President Zhang Zemin and Hu Jintao. It was once Xi Jinping became the President that I decided to gradually pen my thoughts. I observed him and the PLA's modernisation for five years and finally started writing deliberately on the matter after the 19th Chinese Communist Party Congress. Xi also started the military reforms process. The book looks at all these aspects comprehensively.

I would like to acknowledge my gratitude to my mother, wife, son, daughter and their families who gave me the encouragement and support. I wish to acknowledge the support extended to this book by the Vivekananda International Foundation (VIF). A special thanks to the Director, Dr Arvind Gupta, whose writings helped me in my work. Further, Lieutenant General Gautam Bannerjee, the Editor of VIF, was a good sounding board who scrutinised my script and advised me on the current state of PLA modernisation and China's cyber warfare capabilities. Joint Secretary, VIF, Anuttama Ganguly, was instrumental in getting the book printed and selecting the cover as also looking after all administrative details. My grateful thanks also to all of her staff.

21 May 2019   **Major General (Dr) P K Chakravorty, VSM (Retd)**

*

Abbreviations

AA	Anti-Aircraft
AB	Air Borne
AD	Air Defence
ADIZ	Air Defence Identification Zone
AEW&C	Airborne Early Warning and Control
Armd	Armoured
Arty	Artillery
ASAT	Anti Satellite
ASBM	Anti Ship Ballistic Missile
Bde	Brigade
BDR	Border Defence Regiment
BMD	Ballistic Missile Defence
BSM	Battlefield Support Missiles
CBG	Carrier Battle Group
C^4I^2SR	Command, Control, Communications, Computer, Information, Intelligence, Surveillance & Reconnaissance
CMC	Central Military Commission
CNP	Comprehensive National Power
COSTIND	Commission of Science, Technology Industry and National Defence
Div	Division
EEZ	Exclusive Economic Zone
EMP	Electro Magnetic Pulse
E -	Electronic Warfare
Ftr	Fighter
GA	Group Army
Gp	Group
GAD	General Armaments Department
GPD	General Political Department
GLD	General Logistics Department.
HAA	High Altitude Areas.

HOM	High Power Microwave
HQ	Headquarters
IAF	Indian Air Force
ICV	Infantry Combat Vehicle
IED	Improvised Explosive Device
IMF	International Monetary Fund
Inf	Infantry
IOR	Indian Ocean Region
ISIS	Islamic State of Iraq and Syria
JLD	Joint Logistics Department
Kuomintang	Chinese Nationalist Party
LAC	Line of Actual Control
LD	Liaison Department
LC	Line of Control
LWE	Left Wing Extremism
MBT	Main Battle Tank
Mech	Mechanised
MIIT	Ministry of Industry, Information & Technology
MR	Military Region
Msl	Missile
Mtn	Mountain
NCW	Network Centric Warfare
NDSTC	National Defence Science Technology Commission
NDIO	National Defence Industries Office
NLOS	Non-Line of Sight
NPC	National People's Congress
PGM	Precision Guided Munition
PLA	People's Liberation Army
PLAAF	People's Liberation Army Air Force
PLAN	People's Liberation Army Navy
R&D	Research & Development
RDF	Rapid Deployment Force
REMCF	Resolving Emergency Mobile Combat Force
RMA	Revolution In Military Affairs
SATIND	State Administration for Science, Technology, Industry & National Defence

SEZ	Special Economic Zone
Spec Ops	Special Operations
SLOC	Sea Lines Of Communication
SOE	State Owned Enterprises
SRBM	Short Range Ballistic Missiles
UAV	Unmanned Aerial Vehicle
UCAV	Unmanned Combat Aerial Vehicle
US	United States of America

*

List of Tables/Figures

TABLES

FIGURES

*

CHAPTER 1
Prologue

It merits importance that a third of the global population is governed by two Asian capitals—Beijing and New Delhi. Numbers are important in all fields, be it mathematics or economics. The world is facing several challenges. To turn these challenges to opportunities, it is necessary that both countries be a part of the negotiations at the United Nations Security Council (UNSC) or at the International Monetary Fund (IMF) or a part of any economic grouping like the G-15.[1] China and India are certainly the movers and shakers of the 21st century. Undoubtedly, China has taken a lead with its Comprehensive National Power (CNP) growing exponentially. Currently, China is the second largest economy and has the largest armed forces in the world equipped with state-of-the-art weaponry.

The Chinese Communist Party and the Chinese Government have been professing peace throughout their rule. India is also a match to China and is providing a stiff competition in every field. At present China is enjoying 'Shengsi' or a golden era or an age of prosperity after about 300 years. Possibly in about three decades, the Chinese would have the world's largest economy. This is also leading to China emerging as a comprehensive national power. It is extremely important to refer to Paul Kennedy's book, 'The Rise and Fall of Great Powers' here. In this book, he writes, "Long term shifts in economic productivity of nations are co-terminus with the increase or decrease of their global influence.[2] This has been observed in all nations which have rapid growth. Historically, this rise has led to a power struggle and military conflicts."

Ever since its creation, China has been claiming territories of numerous countries. There have been wars and clashes. Further, the tone has remained assertive. To quote an example, the late Mao Zedong, the first Chairman of the People's Republic of China, had after annexing Tibet, described it as China's palm, and Nepal, Sikkim, Bhutan, Arunachal and Ladakh as the country's five fingers. It is pertinent to note that a few maps have shown Assam and the Andaman Islands as a part of China.

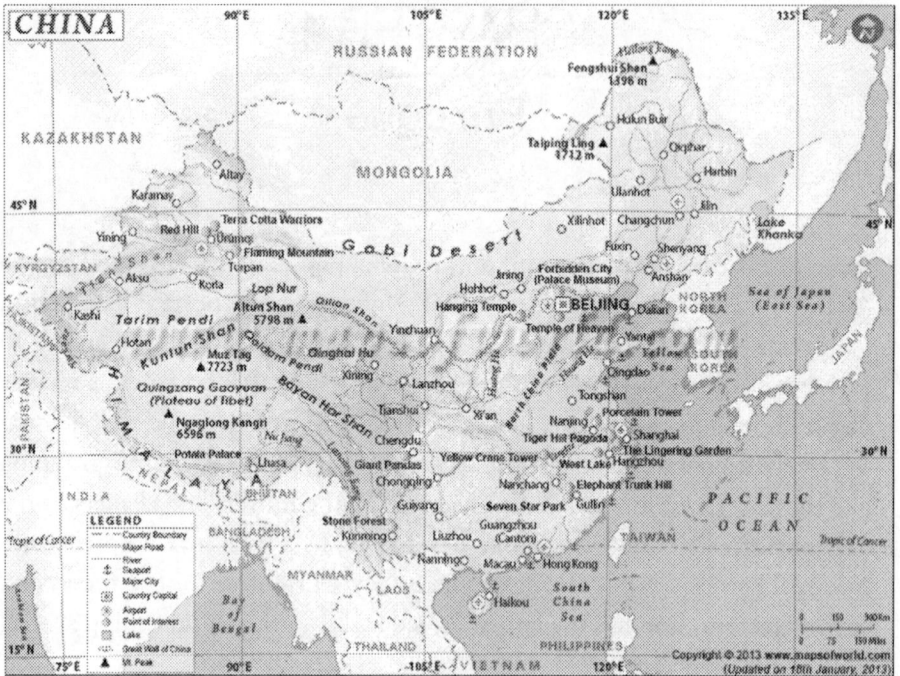

Figure 1.1: Map of China Bordering 14 Countries[3]

Some analysts are of the opinion that China is peace-loving and not greedy for territory. There are others who have a different view. Further, China recognises the McMahon Line as its border with Myanmar but does not recognise the same with India and Bhutan. The correct perception of the Chinese Line of Actual Control (LAC) is unclear, and therefore, this has led to misinterpretation by both countries during patrolling and or implementation of confidence-building measures. Further, there is a surge in Chinese nationalism as demonstrated through its infrastructural innovation, sports and technology which are at levels for the global nations to appreciate.[4] There is an assertiveness to regain sovereignty and status. Further, the Chinese are creating levers of power based on real politick rather than ethics and morality.

Henry Kissinger in his book 'On China', mentions Chinese strategy generally exhibiting three characteristics—meticulous analysis of long-term trends, careful study of tactical options and detailed exploration of operational decisions.[5] The Chinese style of dealing with strategic decisions is undertaken through analysis, careful preparation, attention to psychological and political factors as also the quest for surprise with a conclusion arrived at rapidly. The People's Liberation Army (PLA) of China is closely knit to the Chinese Communist Party. The PLA's modernisation and its rising global status could either make China a more responsible international power or lead to a hardening of its assertive stance, which in turn could further lead to clashes with existing and emerging powers. In order to understand the path China is likely to adopt, it is important to comprehend its defence policy that stems from the modernisation of the PLA.

In India, there has been scant research on the modernisation of the Chinese Armed Forces and its impact on Indian security. The People's Republic of China was established in 1949 under the chairmanship of Mao Zedong. It is one of the oldest civilizations with a 4,500-year-long history filled with military activities. China's traditions with regard to its military have emerged from its strategic concerns, war experience, civil-military relations and technological development. It is pertinent to note that each imperial dynasty and modern government came to power through military struggle. In the twentieth century, the Kuomintang (The Chinese Nationalist Party or KMT) came to power through revolutionary wars against the Qing Dynasty which ruled China from 1644 to 1912. Thereafter, the Chinese Communist Party defeated the KMT through the War for Liberation in 1949. Accordingly, an understanding of Chinese military history is essential for comprehending Chinese civilisation, political institutions and foreign policy.[6]

Communist China emerged in 1949 and the PLA was formed under the Chinese Communist Party (CCP). The PLA obeys the latter's diktat and has proportionate representation in various policy committees. The PLA actively participated in the 'Great Leap Forward', the 'Cultural Revolution' and in Deng Xiaoping's modernisation programmes. Further, it fought the Korean War from 1950 to 1953, the Sino-Indian War of 1962, the Ussuri River Conflict with Russia in 1969 and the Sino-Vietnamese War of 1979. China has not been engaged in a major war for the last 39 years, but the PLA has been involved in skirmishes on the South China Sea, intrusions in the East China Sea and in Tibet, besides preparing for a possible military offensive against Taiwan. China has developed its own defence industry to indigenously produce state-of-the-art weaponry.

Though Chinese White Papers always project a defensive and peaceful attitude, Beijing's intentions appear deceptive. China's official media continues to publicise articles that caution India about China retaining the option of initiating military hostilities. Wen Wei Po, a Hong Kong-based daily owned by the People's Republic of China, with editorial staff from the CCP and controlled by the ruling Politburo Standing Committee, published an article in June 2013, captioned 'Six Wars to be fought by China in the next 50 years'. It was reposted on a Hong Kong web site around the middle of September 2013. The details of the authors' background are yet to be ascertained and contents have been possibly obtained from Chinese defence analysts. The article asserts that China can wipe out past humiliations and regain dignity only after it attains national reunification. The Six Wars visualised are as under:

- Unification of Taiwan which is expected to be fought between 2020 to 2025.
- Capture of Spratly Islands in the South China Sea possibly in the timeline 2025 to 2030.
- Re conquest of Southern Tibet (Arunachal) would possibly be undertaken in the years 2035 to 2040.
- Capture of Diaoyu Island and Ryukyu Island between 2040 and 2045.
- Unification of Outer Mongolia around 2045 to 2050.
- Militarily recapture territory lost to Russia between 2055 and 2060.

The first option deals with Taiwan and states that Taiwan must peacefully unite with China by 2020, failing which, the country should be unified by a war which should take place by 2025. Such a war would be difficult to undertake should there be an intervention by the USA and Japan. The author feels that such a war would last anywhere between three to six months. Post-Taiwan's reunification with China, there would be a lull of about two years, during which China would issue an ultimatum to countries patrolling islands in the South China Sea to withdraw by 2028. These countries would be allowed to preserve their investments followed by withdrawal. China anticipates Vietnam and Philippines to oppose the move with possible assistance from the US. The author says that if concrete results are not attained through negotiations, then the best option is for China to attack Vietnam as it is the most powerful country in the region. Victory over Vietnam would scare the rest. While the war with Vietnam goes on, the other claimants could adopt a wait and watch policy. China is expected to beat Vietnam and establish its suzerainty over the Spratly Islands.

The Third War would be the reconquest of Southern Tibet (Arunachal) between the years 2035 and 2040. The article emphatically states that Arunachal is the only point of conflict between China and India. It further notes the close relations between India, the US, Europe and Russia. It assumes that India would militarily lag behind China during this period. However, a war with India would result in victory after sustaining losses. Accordingly, the best strategy would be to initiate the disintegration of the region. China should leave no stone unturned to instigate Assam and Sikkim to fight for independence. The other option is to provide state-of-the-art weaponry to Pakistan to enable it to capture the Indian part of Kashmir by 2035 and, thereby, give Pakistan control of the entire region. While the fight is on for Kashmir, China should attempt to conquer Arunachal. As per the author, India lacks the capability of fighting a two-front war. If this plan cannot be adopted, the other option is to launch a ground offensive to capture Arunachal (Southern Tibet).[7]

It is pertinent to note that this article may not have emanated from the higher levels of China's military establishment, but it iterates an issue often emphasised by the Chinese media that the country will have to ultimately resort to the use of the PLA to settle border issues. Articles of a similar nature have been appearing in the Chinese press ever since the Review of Asia policy was undertaken in 2011. A publication of the official China mouthpiece in November 2011 recommended that China adopt new approaches in dealing with its neighbours. It further stated that goodwill may not bring harmony and sometimes certain altercations with neighbours are appropriate and can result in the return of peace.[8] Accordingly, a study on this subject is necessary.

The main objective of the book is to assess the impact of the modernization of the Chinese military on India's security. The objectives are:

- To analyse Chinese military modernisation and capabilities.
- To identify the strengths of the Chinese defence industry and compare Indian capabilities.
- To study Chinese armed forces weaknesses which India could suitably exploit.

- To assess impact of China's emergence as a strong military and economic power globally.
- To analyse security implications due to China's rise as a comprehensive national power.
- India has grown and can counter any Chinese military offensive with precision.

NOTES

1. William Antholis, "Inside Out India and China", Local Politics Go Global, *Brookings Institute*, Washington D.C., 2013, p.1.
2. Paul Kennedy, "The Rise and fall of Great Powers", Random House, USA, 1987, pp 438-439.
3. Map of China bordering 14 countries at www.mapsofworld.com updated 18 January 2013.
4. General V P Malik, "Foreword: China's Defence Policy, Indian Perspective", *KW Publishers Private Limited*, New Delhi, 2011, pp ix-x.
5. Henry Kissinger, "On China", *Penguin Press*, USA, 2011.
6. Xiaobing Li, "China at War: An Encyclopedia", *Pentagon Press*, New Delhi, 2012.
7. Translated from a Hong Kong blog, *Midnight Express* 2046 (ME 2046), 2013.
8. Jayadeva Ranade, "Dreaming Big", *Institute of Peace and Conflict Studies*, 07 October 2013.

*

CHAPTER 2

Existing Published Material on the Issues

The Defence White Paper is the main document on security brought out by China's defence ministry since 1995, but in spite of it, the PLA remains an enigma for the entire world. White Papers issued between 1995 to 2015 remain silent on several issues, forcing professionals to ascertain veracity through a combination of facts and demonstrated behaviour. Therefore, it is important to review the past, examine the present and analyse future projections and their impact on India. This research aims at filling these gaps to determine actions to be taken for rectification. Currently, we are not clear of China's capabilities or intentions and an analysis of these issues is imperative for India's national security.

Xiaobing Li, in his book, 'China at War: An Encyclopedia', points out that China is one of the oldest civilisations with a recorded military history of 4500 years. It is pertinent to note that based on its unique geographic setting, demographic characteristics and political structure, China's military tradition emerged from its strategic concerns, war experience, civil-military relations and technological development. China is the largest country in Asia, both as per population and territory. Further, the Chinese have often been involved in border conflicts, territorial expansion, civil wars and military invasions. It is indeed true that China's war-fighting experience has been intertwined with Chinese history. It is pertinent to note that each imperial dynasty and government came to power through military struggle. It is interesting that in the twentieth century the Chinese Nationalist Party or the Kuomintang (KMT) came to power through revolutionary wars against the Qing Dynasty which ruled between 1644 and 1912. The KMT fought the warlords from 1916 to 1927. Similarly, the Chinese Communist Party defeated the KMT through the Chinese Civil War between 1946 and 1949 and established the People's Republic of China (PRC). A study of Chinese military history is essential for making a correct assessment of Chinese thought processes, political institutions, foreign and defence policies.[1] The book would analyse these aspects in detail to arrive at suitable deductions.

Major General G D Bakshi, in his book, 'The Sino-Vietnam War of 1979', refers to Deng Xiao Ping coming to power and making China attack Vietnam in 1979 'to teach a lesson' to the latter. The Vietnamese held their ground and only the Chinese learnt a few lessons.[2] It is to be observed that Deng consolidated his position as the leader of China by undertaking this offensive, though the results were unspectacular. The PLA suffered huge losses. The Gulf War which liberated Kuwait in 1990-91 shook the PLA and compelled it to undertake a revolution in military affairs. China crafted a grand strategy as per which it would become the Asia-Pacific region's dominant economic and military power during the 2010-2015 period and a major power by 2040. In a RAND study, Michael Swaine and Ashley Tellis are of the view that China's strategic objective aims to achieve the following interrelated objectives:[3]

- The preservation of the domestic order and its wellbeing in the face of different forms of social strife;
- Defence against persistent external threats to national sovereignty and territory;
- The attainment of geopolitical influence as a major and perhaps, primary state.

John Wilson Lewis and Xue Litai, in their book, 'China's Search for a Modern Air Force', bring out China's ignominious exit from Vietnam in 1979 and maintain that the end of the Gulf War saw a change from "The Doctrine of People's War to People's War under Modern Conditions", which was introduced in 1993. The PLA deduced that "Big Peace" at the geo-strategic level could not prevent local or small wars at the regional level. Accordingly, the PLA graduated to thinking and fighting local or limited wars with a focus on small-scale conflicts restricted to the territorial borders, conflict over territorial seas, surprise air attacks, defence against deliberate attacks into own territory and punitive counter-attacks into enemy territory to oppose invasion.[4]

The Beijing Military Science Publishing House has published books on Chinese strategy transformation from the "People's War" to "Active Defence". David Shambaugh in his Asian Security Series has also mentioned these issues.

China has currently moved onto the strategy of Active Defence which is undertaking local wars under hi-tech conditions. The doctrine calls for integrated deep strikes on the enemy's firepower capabilities. Further, it calls for forward positioning, frontier defence, engagement of the enemy at or over the border and potential engagement in conflict beyond China's immediate periphery.[5] It is pertinent to note that though all Chinese White Papers profess a strategic adherence to self defence, the PLA National Defence University (NDU) textbook titled "The Science of Campaigns", as brought out in the US Department of Defence PLA Report, says the essence of Active Defence is to take the initiative and annihilate the enemy.[6] This is further clarified in another PLA book titled 'The Science of Military Strategy' which notes 'Under high tech conditions', for the defensive side, the strategy of gaining mastery by striking only after the enemy has struck does not mean waiting for the enemy's strike passively. Thereafter it fundamentally transforms the definition of first shot by stating, "Hostile forces such as religious extremists, national separatists and international terrorists challenged a country's sovereignty, it could be considered as firing the first shot on the plane of politics and strategy."[7] In simplistic terms, taking an offensive stance is termed as Active Defence. The book will focus on these issues.

Richard Fisher's book, 'China's Military Modernisation, Building for Regional and Global Research', covers the technical aspects of Chinese modernisation. However, there are gaps in the need, as also the implications. China's military modernisation can be broadly divided into two phases. The first phase commenced from the era of Deng Xiao Ping, probably up to the first part of 2010 and the second phase followed thereafter. The first phase can be termed as the catch-up period to prepare for large regional military contingencies such as Taiwan and consolidation of control over the South China Sea. The second period builds on the accomplishments of the first phase with greater emphasis on exercising global influence. The areas focused were Doctrine, Military Industrial Sector and the introduction of Information Warfare.[8]

The book, 'Firepower 2030', covers nuances of military modernisation. China's military modernisation has resulted in it having the largest armed forces in the world. With a current stated defence budget of about $160 billion, the Chinese armed forces are modernising exponentially and, by 2030, would possibly be close to the United States in state-of-the art weaponry. This has to be viewed against the backdrop of China's defence preparedness with that of the United States which is its sole strategic competitor. Its defence industry, with its focus on aerospace, shipbuilding, nanotechnology and direct energy weapons, would catapult it into a higher league of indigenous manufacture by 2030. The focus of China is on integrating technology and using the asymmetry to its advantage by developing specialised missiles like the anti-ship missile for engaging aircraft carrier group task forces, special forces, stealth fighters, Submarine Launched Ballistic Missiles (SLBMs), competent Information Warriors, satellites providing navigation systems, and finally, a space station enabling research in the fields of astronomy, surveillance systems and possibly space-based weapons. China's present and future leaders all comprise technocrats who are leaving no stone unturned to bridge the technology gap with the United States and this would automatically put them ahead of the United States.[9]

The present military structure was created by Deng Xiao Ping in 1980. This has been covered in the book by Colonel RSN Singh, 'China's Asian Strategic and Military Perspective'. However, the capabilities resulting from the Force Structure needs to be analysed. The same would be undertaken in the ensuing portions of the book. The Chinese Armed Forces comprise the PLA, People's Armed Police Force (PAPF) and the militia. The PLA comprises the Army, Navy, Air Force and the Second Artillery. The organisations are undergoing transformations as per the directions of President Xi Jinping and are likely to be completed by 2020. The PAPF is responsible for the maintenance of internal security, law and order and to keep the country free from social disturbance. The PLA had seven Military Regions (MRs) which are being transformed into five theatre commands. The Navy and Air Force are officially designated as the PLA Navy (PLAN) and the PLA Air Force (PLAAF). The Second Artillery is linked with the employment of convention and nuclear missiles. It is now being designated as the PLA Rocket Force. The Central Military Commission (CMC) exercises command and control over the armed forces and is directly under the Chinese Communist Party (CCP). The CMC Chairman is the commander of the armed forces. The Chinese Ministry of Defence does not exercise direct control over the PLA and is entrusted with the responsibility of the defence industry, construction of military facilities and foreign relationships.[10] The CMC, which is under the party, controls the armed forces and is accountable to the Communist Party.

The PLA's ground force of 2.25 million makes it the largest army in the world. There are 18 corps-sized Group Armies which act as the PLA's strike element in offensive operations. There are 21 Rapid Reaction Force (RRF) Divisions and 3 Airborne Divisions under the PLAAF. The PLAN is aiming for blue water capability by 2030. While it may not attain the global force level of the US Navy, it would pose asymmetric threats like the development of steep dive anti-aircraft carrier missiles which would pose threats to carrier task forces. Air Commodore Ramesh Phadke, in his book, covers the nuances of the PLAAF. The PLAAF is the third largest air force in the world and started modernising after the Second Gulf War. They are gradually moving from quantity to quality. They have developed the J-10 fighter which is a copy of the Israeli Lavi class fighter and are currently in the process of developing two Fifth Generation Fighter Aircrafts (FGFA), the J-20 and the J-31. The Air Force is also in possession of advanced S-300 PMU2 Anti-Aircraft Defence Systems with a range of 150 km. Currently, they have acquired the S 400 Surface to Air Missile systems. They are also acquiring AWACs and superior command and control systems. The Second Artillery Corps is the strategic missile force of the People's Republic of China. China has numerous missiles of all types and is capable of launching from air, sea and subsurface. China has also dominated outer space. On 11 January, 2007, China launched an anti-satellite rocket that intercepted and physically destroyed an ageing weather satellite. Apart from this, it has developed the Beidou Navigation System and is developing a direct energy weapon system.[11]

There are limited explanations in the available literature on Chinese capabilities and intentions. The Chinese annual military budget is stated to be $160 billion, which is about three-and-a-half times India's defence budget. While China's professed intentions may be peaceful, its overwhelming military capabilities permit it to change to suit its political needs. The Chinese have been involved in four major wars since the Communist Party took charge. There are distinctive information gaps which led to these wars. Surprisingly, estimates of Chinese involvement were incorrect in all wars except the 1979 war with Vietnam. Analysis of Chinese military capabilities is a must to understand their perceived intention. Similarly, India needs to carefully assess

Chinese capabilities and deduce its intentions. We have an unsettled border with China with the latter staking a claim to Arunachal Pradesh which it refers as Southern Tibet. China also occupies Aksai Chin and the Shaksgam Valley which India claims. There are three drivers which could lead to a possible conflict. The first would be Chinese Regime Stability and Nationalism, the Tibet factor and internal developments in Arunachal Pradesh. The scenarios could ascendant India and assertive China. The application of drivers to these scenarios could lead to a full spectrum conflict unless necessary measures are taken by India. China has recently made forays in the Indian Ocean which could lead to posturing and conflict in the immediate future.

A correct assessment of PLA modernisation would lead us to a need for India to view her problems with China seriously as these could blow up to multiple intrusions, use of cyber warfare and an overwhelming use of firepower, including missiles, anti-satellite or direct energy weapons. These could be done sporadically or as a well-orchestrated operation of the war. India certainly needs to dissuade China from undertaking such adventures. The first step is for the government is to have a national security strategy to deal with collusive threats from Pakistan or China. The next is to modernise our armed forces for fighting this two-front war. The third is that we must induct and operationalise the Agni missile and the BrahMos missile on the Sino-Indian border within the next five years. In short, we must have both conventional and nuclear deterrence against China. The fourth aspect is to complete the construction of the 72 roads leading to India's border with China by 2025. The fifth is we must tell China that our recognition of Tibet as a part of China is contingent on Beijing recognising Arunachal Pradesh as a part of our country. The sixth issue is to exploit Chinese vulnerability on movement of resources across the Indian Ocean. The seventh aspect is to increase our defence partnership with Japan, Vietnam and the United States. The eighth and final aspect is to have robust border negotiations.

There are gaps in the perception of China as very few analysts study the latter's military capabilities thoroughly. The PLA is answerable to the Communist Party, which would like to legitimise its authoritarian rule by assertively dominating Asia. Indications of the Chinese ADIZ and the establishment of an oil rig in the Paracel Islands are pointers in this direction. The research will focus on these areas to comprehend Chinese intentions and its implications on India's national security. The aforesaid review of literature clearly indicates that writers have concentrated on various dimensions and components of Chinese capability. The existing knowledge gap suggests that an exclusive study is needed to address it.

Research Gaps

Chinese military modernisation has been undertaken after the First Gulf War in 1990, but no country took a serious note of it as the focus was on the economic build-up of the country which almost grew at 10 per cent for a considerable period of time. From the literature examined the following gaps were discerned:

- There are few research publications which focus on the scale of the PLA's modernization;
- There is no formal research on the strength of the Chinese defence industrial base;
- There is no comprehensive analysis on China's assertiveness or its impact on global security;
- There is no comprehensive study on the security implications for India;
- There is no study on measures to be taken to improve India's defence preparedness in the face of Chinese assertiveness.

Visualisation

China has undertaken four modernisations under former leader Deng Xiao Ping. As on date, the country is the world's second largest economy and largest armed force. It is assumed that China would build up its military power holistically to be a global player. The following are assumed:

- Assumption One: The modernisation process of the PLA to be completed by 2030;
- Assumption Two: Building a defence industrial complex in China to allow indigenous weapons production.

All this would enable China to have a modern army, a blue water navy and an air force by 2030 capable of dominating areas of conflict. Developments would also take place in the Second Artillery; Outer Space and Direct Energy weapons.[12] China has also floated the concept of One Belt One Road which would improve its connectivity with the extended neighbourhood. This modernisation is likely to result in greater capabilities, which in turn will lead to greater ambitions. Further, China is becoming assertive over its disputes with Taiwan, Japan, Vietnam, Philippines and India. These countries have to respond as China is bound to have domestic problems like slower economic growth, which could be tranquilised by external arm twisting by its military.

The moot question is whether China is seeking a peaceful rise or is it going to undertake offensive action to occupy these disputed areas? Current trends indicate a rise in assertiveness, be it the declaration of the ADIZ or the May 2014 placement of a mobile oil rig by 80 PLAN ships with air cover in the proximity of Paracel Islands resulting in a maritime standoff with Vietnam. Further, China has been reclaiming land and building airstrips in the South China Sea. India has undergone numerous transgressions, the major ones being the incident in the Eastern Ladakh region in September 2014 during the visit of President Xi Jinping and the Doklam standoff which lasted from June 16, 2017 to August 28, 2017. China has said the border dispute will take some time to resolve. Its military modernisation and equipping Pakistan with nuclear weapons poses a direct threat to India. The modernisation of its capabilities will enable it to launch a full spectrum offensive against India. India, on its part, being a democratic country, will need more time to respond to the PLA assertiveness.

There is a school of thought that says nuclear weapons negate the possibility of India and China engaging in a major war. Even in such an eventuality limited wars and their modern variations cannot be ruled out. In such a case, China is likely to use cyber warfare, anti-satellite weapons, missiles, overwhelming firepower and possibly a ground offensive comprising multiple options. This possibly calls for India to undertake the following measures:

- Need for National Security Strategy and a strategic response to China by intensifying strategic partnerships with the US, Japan, Vietnam, Australia and Russia.
- Build up our Comprehensive National Power.
- Joint operations in network centric conditions.
- Modernise our armed forces to face dual threats from China and Pakistan.
- Reorganise our DRDO to focus only on cutting edge technologies.
- Create a level-playing field between defence public sector units and the private sector.

- Develop pockets of excellence by focusing on asymmetric warfare, cyber warfare and assassins mace weapons.
- Create a diplomatic strategy to win war and ensure peace.

A detailed research would enable us to ascertain issues and chalk out strategies to meet China's assertiveness. India is currently strong and China would have to think hard before having a military contest. The Chinese are certainly not ten feet tall and India is capable of giving a fitting reply. But there are the following constraints:

- The analysis is based on perceptions available in the limited literature on the subject. Accordingly logical deductions are based on available data.
- Data available in the classified domain has is referred so that there is no jeopardy of security interests.
- Changing the political dynamics in China, India and the United States would take some time. Consequently, there could be a relative change in the overall situation in the region.

NOTES

1. Xiao Bing Li, "China at War An Encyclopedia", *Pentagon Press*, New Delhi, 2012, page xv. Major General G D Bakshi, "The Sino Vietnam War 1979",Case Studies in Limited Wars, *Bharat Rakshak Monitor*-Volume 3, 2000, p.3.
2. Michael D.Swaine and Ashley J. Tellis, "Interpreting China's Grand Strategy: Past, Present and Future", *RAND*: Santa Monica, CA 2000, p.x.
3. John Wilson Lewis and Xue Litai, "China's Search for a Modern Air Force", *International Security, Volume-24, No 1 (Summer 1999)*, p.29.
4. David Shambaugh, "China's CBMs in the Region", *Asian Security Series, Henry L. Stimson Centre*, Washington D.C. December 1996.
5. US Department of Defence, "PLA Report", 2007, pp 12-13.
6. Peng Guangqian and Yao Youzhi, "The Science of Military Strength", *Beijing Military Science Publish*ing House, 2005, p.426.
7. Richard D. Fisher Jr, "China's Military Modernization, Building for Regional and Global Research", *Pentagon Press*, New Delhi, 2009, p.67.
8. P K Chakravorty, "Firepower 2030", *KW Publishers Private Limited*, New Delhi, 2013, p.49.
9. Col RSN Singh, "China Asian Strategic and Military Perspective (Observer Research Foundation)", *Lancers Publishers and Distributors*, New Delhi, 2005, pp42-44.
10. Air Cmde Ramesh V Phadke, "Defending Indian Skies against the PLAAF", *Indian Defence Review*, January-March 2012, pp. 39.
12. Colonel Mick Ryan, "India China in 2030,"*Australian Defence Forces Journal*, Issue No 88, July-August 2012, pp 44-56.

CHAPTER 3

Modernisation of PLA

Transformation under Deng Xiaoping

Mao expired on September 9, 1976. A power struggle ensued after his death. In July 1977, with the backing of the moderate military leadership, Deng Xiaoping reassumed his position as PLA Chief of General Staff and head of other party and state posts. Deng also became Vice Chairman of the Central Military Commission (CMC). It was during this period that Vietnam attacked Cambodia and Deng strongly supported the idea of teaching Vietnam a lesson by launching an offensive with 25 divisions. The war revealed the weakness of the PLA and resulted in Deng initiating his four modernisations in which defence formed an important component. The restructuring and modification of the PLA commenced immediately to be able to fight the People's War under modern conditions. The reorganisation led to the beginning of combined arms and joint service exercises and the commencement of new procurement programmes.[1]

Figure 3.1: Deng Xiaoping the Visionary Leader[2]

While Deng went about restructuring the PLA, changes in its weaponry were at best marginal. The First Gulf War in 1991 was a wake-up call for the Chinese as they were left astounded by the 500 new technologies developed by the US in the 1980s and thereafter unleashed. China took a decision to invoke a Revolution in Military Affairs (RMA). Prior to this, the Chinese armed forces had obsolete equipment that needed modernisation. Essential aspects of the RMA are as elucidated. First of all, RMAs concern significant progress and change in at least five important military-related areas which comprise technology, systems, operations, organisation and strategy. The second aspect is that a synergistic combination of these developments forms the true RMA and alters the nature of warfare. The third aspect deals with the emergence of RMA due to revolutionary changes within the broader social, economic and political environment. The fourth aspect pertains to the smooth and successful process of recognition, appreciation and exploitation of RMA made possible through flexibility, acceptability, innovation and openness to change.[3]

The elements of the current RMA are:

- The first issue deals with changes in the tools of war. This would entail Information Dominance or Command, Control, Communications Computer, Information, Intelligence, Surveillance and Reconnaissance (C^4I^2SR) as also Long Range Precision Strike, Sensor to shooter links and a Global Positioning System.
- The second issue pertains to changes in military behaviour. This applies to joint doctrine and operations, force synergies, decentralisation of powers and creation of knowledge warriors.
- The third issue deals with changes in the nature of warfare. This would configure cyber war to include strategic information attack, nonlinear warfare, fourth dimensional warfare and high technology as well as low intensity warfare.[4]

The Chinese RMA has nine distinct components:

- The first and foremost objective is to downsize the PLA and improve its quality;
- The second is to strengthen the Second Artillery to improve its strategic reach and power projection capabilities;
- The third is speeding up information capabilities to make the PLA a knowledge-age force ;
- The fourth pertains to accelerating the modernisation of weaponry and equipment;

- The fifth aspect relates to improving the quality of military personnel to meet the needs of knowledge-age warfare;
- The sixth is to enhance joint operational and training capabilities;
- The seventh relates to the speeding up of logistic reforms;
- The eighth is to emphasize the importance of political work contribution towards enhancing combat;
- The ninth and the last aspect is to govern the armed forces according to law.

Changing Organisations and Equipment

Along with modernisation, the force structure of the PLA saw the creation of the Rapid Reaction Force (RRF). Rapid reaction in the PLA means that all major elements being deployed to any part of China within two weeks. The 15 Air Borne Corps located at Wuhan is a part of the PLA Air Force (PLAAF). It comprises of three paratrooper divisions, each having three paratrooper regiments and a light artillery regiment. This is earmarked as RRF in addition to the mechanised elements from other regions.[5]

Future inductions in the army primarily concern small arms, anti-armour weapons, armour, armoured personnel carriers and artillery. In as much as small arms are concerned, the Chinese experimented with various calibres between 5.5 and 6 mm before deciding on the 5.8 mm as the standard small arms calibre. This is known as the Type 87 Assault Rifle, with a bull-pup design. It can be modified to carry a grenade launcher. As regards anti-armour weapons, this has been a weak point in the PLA Armoury. There are broadly four types. However, the Red Arrow Weapon Guided System, a second generation guided missile system intended for an anti-armour role with a range of 4000 metres, is the most improved weapon system. It is a crew portable weapon fired from a ground tripod mount and can be configured for mounting in or on a variety of wheeled or tracked vehicles. It is also mounted on the Harbin Z-9 G helicopter which is used by PLA aviation units as an attack helicopter. It is similar in appearance to the Milan System. As regards armour, the most advanced PLA Main Battle Tank is the Type 99, based on the Russian T-72 chassis. Type 99, tank was first introduced in 1999. Eighty of these tanks were inducted by 2006. This has a 125 mm smooth-bore gun which can fire an Israeli assisted M711 shell with an armour penetration of 850 mm. It is the only tank in the world equipped with laser sensor damage weapon which is capable of destroying the optical instrument of the enemy tank as also having the ability to blind the crew. The gun can be fired manually and with the aid of computers. The tank's welded turret is of angular design, with spaced modular armour and control panels. The frontal armour is capable of M1 Abrams of the United States.

The Chinese have fabricated APCs based on the BMP-2. The North China Industries Corporation (NORINCO) announced that it had developed the Type 90 APC family which consists of ten variants. This has also been referred to by some Chinese sources as the Type 91 APC. Based on the variant the engine is a 320 HP or 360 HP diesel engine. With a crew of two, the APC has a troop complement of 13. The variants are the Infantry Combat Vehicle, Anti-tank Missile Launcher, Tracked Armoured Command Vehicle, 82 mm Self Propelled Mortar, 120 mm Self-propelled Mortar, 122mm Self Propelled Howitzer,130 mm Self Propelled Rocket Launcher, Tracked Armoured Ambulance and Tracked Armoured Recovery Vehicle.[7]

The conventional artillery is based on the Type 59-1,130 mm field gun. The 152 mm is a medium gun. Further, the 105 mm and the 122mm constitute the basic calibre for light and mountain formations. The 122 mm and 152 mm guns have self-propelled versions in their group armies that have mechanised formations in their ORB. The PLZ-05 is a self-propelled Howitzer with a 52 calibre barrel and with an extended range. Its full bore ammunition reaches a range of 50 km. As on date, the PLA has about 300 guns. China has claimed that the WS-35 ammunition of this gun can fire up to a range of 100 km. This could be a typing error and is impracticable given the characteristics of this weapon. The 130 mm field gun is being replaced by a Type 88, 155 mm, which is a towed version of the PLZ-05. There are reports that the 155 mm has been developed with technology from Austria. China has developed and inducted a state-of-the-art Multiple Launcher Rocket System (MLRS), A-100, which is similar to the Smerch and has a range of 80 km. The Chinese are in the process of developing an advanced version with an enhanced range of 180 km. Further, the Chinese Precision Machinery Import and Export Corporation ATN has developed a long-range unguided artillery rocket system called the M-18. According to available information, this rocket system has a diameter of 350 mm, carries a 100 to 150 kilogram conventional warhead and is capable of firing up to a range of between 80 to 100 km. All this makes Chinese artillery a veritable versatile firepower component that can destroy targets effectively.[8]

The PLA Navy (PLAN) is aiming for blue water capability which would take place by 2030. While it may not attain the global force level of the US Navy, it would be able to pose asymmetric threats like induction of steep dive anti-ship missiles which would pose threats to Carrier Battle Groups. The PLAN has three fleets. The North Sea Fleet with its headquarters at Qingdao undertakes the offshore active defence of the Yellow China Sea. The East Sea Fleet has headquarters at Dongqain Lake with its focus on the East China Sea and finally, the South Sea Fleet which has its headquarters at Zhangjiang, has a crucial task in furthering China's claims in the South China Sea. Its ships comprise one aircraft carrier (presently undergoing operational sea trials), three nuclear powered ballistic missile submarines (SSBN), two Jia class and one Xia class submarines capable of firing SLBMs. In addition, China has seven nuclear-powered submarines, 76 other submarines, 27 destroyers, 35 frigates, 19 Landing Ship Transport (LST), 346 patrol vessels and numerous minesweepers as also auxiliary ships.[9] Naval assets of the PLAN have been steadily increasing, leading to a combination of aircraft and helicopters. The current inventory constitutes 22 Sukhoi 30 Mark II and 165 fighter bombers which are capable of striking ships, 715 fighters capable of ground attack strikes, 24 maritime reconnaissance aircraft with capabilities for Anti-Submarine Warfare (ASW), helicopters and also transport aircraft. By 2030, China will possibly have three aircraft carriers and a modernised navy capable of patrolling the Indian Ocean, the seas bordering China and gradually navigating into Western Pacific. Normally it takes about 20 years for a navy to acquire the skills to operationalise an aircraft carrier, but the Chinese have used modern methods to reduce the gestation period.

The PLA Air Force (PLAAF) is the third largest air force in the world and genuinely started modernising after the First Gulf War. The use of air power is indispensable despite China becoming a nuclear power. The shock and awe created by the US Air Force woke the PLAAF, and thereafter, it has modernised at an incredible pace. It was at that time that the Soviet Union broke up and Russia was plagued with serious difficulties. China with a sound economy signed a major deal for the purchase of 24 SU-27 (equivalent to the US, F-15 class), with a provision for the local manufacture of another 200 aircraft. China also purchased large numbers of the Rolls Royce Spey-200 engines from the UK for the locally developed JH 7/FB 7 fighter bombers. Further, it accessed technology from Israel and also purchased the Russian aero engines, the RD 93 and AI 31F, to kick start two other local fighter programmes. The result was the JF-17 Thunder which was jointly produced with Pakistan and the J-10 based on the Israeli designer fighter, the Lavi of the F-16 class. Israel has been compelled to give up the Lavi programme under pressure from the US. It is of interest to note that Pakistan has supplied a crashed F-16 and a dud air-launched Tomahawk Cruise missile to China for reverse engineering. The Chinese are attempting to copy the AI-31 turbofan engine that powers the SU-30 and this is a difficult task which would be completed shortly. At their level, they have produced the WZ-10 attack helicopter which is producing reasonable results. Other modifications in the Chinese PLAAF include a modification of the AN-12 with advanced avionics into an Airborne Early Warning and Control (AEW&C) aircraft. The H-6 (the Chinese version of the 1950 vintage TU-16 bomber) has been modified with the more powerful Russian D-30 KP engine and is still operational. These aircraft have multifarious uses and are used for light refuelling, electronic surveillance and to deliver anti-ship cruise missiles from safe standoff distances. The Chinese have also tested two Fifth Generation Fighter Aircrafts, the J-20 and the J-31. While the J-20 has similarities to the US F-35, the J-31 is almost akin to the F-22 Raptor. The J-20 is being developed by Chengdu Aircraft, whereas the J-31 is being developed by aircraft industries at Shenyang. Both are twin-engine stealth aircraft that would add tremendous capabilities to the PLAAF. It is anticipated that both these aircraft would take at least five years for induction.[10]

According to the Military Balance 2011, the PLAAF has about 1687 aircraft. The Chinese are capable of manufacturing 40 to 50 combat aircraft every year. They also have about 550 transport aircraft. The aircraft are grouped into 45 divisions, each having three regiments. Each regiment has three squadrons and each squadron has three flights, with each flight having three to four aircraft. China has also introduced UAVs and Unmanned Combat Aerial Vehicles (UCAVs). The UAVs are the ASN 105, 229 A, Japanese RMAX, Shenyang BA-5 and WZ-5. The Unmanned Combat Aerial Vehicles (UCAVs) are the Israeli Harpy, Pterodactyl, Pterosaur, WJ-600 and CH-3. These are capable of surveillance, engagement of targets and Post Strike Damage Assessment (PSDA). The PLAAF has no combat experience nor has it participated in exercises with air forces other than a few aircraft in Turkey in 2011. Currently, its equipment is by and large of the second, third as also fourth generation aircraft, accelerating its indigenous development capability. As described, the variety of weapon systems capable of being delivered from the air makes it on par with other air forces in the employment of air power.[11] Like the Chinese Navy, the Chinese Air Force has recently been exercising with the Russians to hone up its skills.

The Second Artillery Corps (now known as the PLA Rocket Force) is the strategic missile force of the People's Republic of China. The Second Artillery was established on July 1, 1966, and made its first public appearance on October 1, 1984. The operational headquarters is located at Qinghe. The Corps is under the direct command of the Chinese Central Military Commission. Further, it operates both conventional and nuclear missiles. The exact number of nuclear warheads held by China is not known but it is estimated to be around 200 to 250.[12] China possesses one of the largest land-based missile forces in the world. The country is capable of inundating the region with its ballistic and cruise missiles. China fired its first ICBM in 1980. The DF-5 is capable of engaging targets in both the US and Russia. In 1981, China launched three satellites from a single vehicle thereby attaining the capability of launching Multiple Independent Reentry Vehicles (MIRVs). By 1986, China developed a credible nuclear deterrence with capability for engagement from land, sea and air. The Chinese land-based missile force comprises 38 operational units. There are possibly eight units supporting ICBMs and the remaining are mobile theatre-based systems. Each unit is organised at an operational base. Missiles are based in six bases in different geographic locations. Each base has numerous subordinate missile brigades and field launch pads. It is extremely difficult to identify these launch pads and normally a hard concrete pad is associated with missile launching position. It is found that for the DF-11, the length of the pad is 15 metres, for the DF-15 it is 26metres and for the DF-21 it is 45 metres.

The missile bases are located on the basis of their strategic requirement. The 51st base, consisting of six missile bases in North Eastern China, faces South-East Russia, South Korea and Japan. The 52nd base, comprising of 12 missile battalions in South East China, faces Taiwan. The 53rd base, consisting of four missile battalions in Southern China, faces Vietnam and possibly Tibet at extreme ranges. The 54th base has six missile battalions in Eastern China catering for Taiwan, Southern Japan and the southern part of the Republic of Korea. The 55th missile base has two missile battalions in Southern China targeting Tibet and Vietnam. Finally, the 56th missile base is formed of eight battalions in Northern China mainly catering for targets in Russia. These units are extremely flexible and except for limited numbers in silos, can be moved to different locations by road or rail.[13]

Flight at lowermost altitude making it hard for air defence means to kill the missile

Target approach from preset direction by-passing islands and air defence zones

Penetrating high-explosive WH blasting at an optimum depth

Figure 3.2: Chinese Missile[14]

Currently, the Chinese missile inventory comprises of a variety of ballistic and cruise missiles. Essential missiles are the DF-2 (CSS-2) with a range of 2650 km, DF-4 (CSS-3) ranging 2200-km, the modified DF-5A(CSS-4, Mod-2) an ICBM with MIRV attaining a maximum range of 13000-km, DF-21A (CSS-5, Mod-2) with a range of 2150-km, DF-15C (CSS-6, Mod-3, modified M-9) attaining a range of 750-km, DF-11A (CSS-7, Mod-2, modified M-11) with a maximum range of 500-km, JL-2 (CSS NX-14) attaining a range of 7,200-km, DF-31(CSS-10, Mod-1) with a range of 8000-km and finally DF-31 A (CSS-10-Mod-2) with a range of 11,200-km and with MIRV capability. On July 24, 2012, China tested its new DF-41, ICBM with a range of 15,000-km that can cover the entire USA. China has modified the DF-21D with possibly a steep dive capability for engagement of ships. China has numerous cruise missiles which are the SY-1, HY, FL, YJ, C 701, C 801 and these have a range between 300 to 600 km. There are about 650 DF-11A (M-11) and DF-15C (M-9) missiles deployed opposite Taiwan. There are several DF-4 and DF-21A medium-range missiles that can target India, Russia and Japan. There are about 18 to 24 DF-5A which can reach locations in Europe and the United States. China is in the process of deploying the newly developed DF-31 A and the JL-2 against any worthwhile target. The Chinese artillery has the flexibility of changing the quantum of missiles against any target with ease and confidence. Further, China has moved to solid propellants with respect to the DF-11A, DF-15A, DF-21A, DF-21 D, DF-31 A, DF-41 and JL-2.[15] PLA Rocket Forces are under the Central Authority, but the missiles being dispersed to various theatre commands, ipso facto come under the local administration under the Headquarters Theatre Command. This permits the theatre commander to influence aspects as operationally required.

Deng Xiao Ping had successfully introduced technology into the PLA. High technology research has resulted in the development of weaponry in diverse fields. It is a long-standing practice in Chinese statecraft, going back thousands of years to seek a trump card or "Assassins Mace" weapons against the adversary. These are high technology weapons which would surprise and defeat the enemy. The National Defence University and all organs dealing with weapons development have focused on high technology weapons. It is pertinent to note a statement by Major General Wang Hongguang, Commandant of the PLA Armoured Forces Engineering Academy.[16] "Extending our vision to the 21st century, the extensive application of information technology, nanotechnology, new materials technology, new energy resources technology as also other high and new technologies will enable our army to be reborn. Operational space will become even wider, operational modes will become more varied, response time will become even quicker, actions will be more agile and attacks will become more forceful. All types of weapon systems, support and logistics systems will combine with the information flow to become one entity, implementing real coordination of high efficiency and accuracy, real-time attack and real-time support. Electro-magnetic artillery, kinetic bombs of high altitude, high speed as also smart weapons and high-efficiency pulse weapons with laser and particle beam capabilities will through their unique capabilities release the operational capabilities and threat capacity of the ground forces. The mass tactics of larger infantry operations will only remain in people's memories."

In terms of high technology weapon system, China is developing lasers, radio frequency, thermo-baric, electromagnetic, nano, biotechnical, stealth hypersonic and super-cavitating underwater weapons. A laser is being developed for communications, radar applications and thermal kill weapons. As per the US Department of Defence, China possibly has the capability to damage under specific conditions the optical sensors on satellites that are vulnerable to lasers. Further, it is reported that the focus is to utilise lasers for the destruction of personnel, precision guidance munitions, Air Defence weapons and satellites. In addition, lasers are being developed to arm UAVs, satellites and cannons. Further, they are being tried out for underwater communications. The Chinese have been contemplating placing lasers in outer space for degradation and destruction of satellites.

Taiwanese sources have reported that the PLA was nearing the deployment of a new non-nuclear Electro Magnetic Pulse (EMP) warhead on a Short Range Ballistic Missile (SRBM). This is a High Power Microwave (HPM) warhead fitted on to a new version of the SRBM. EMP and HPM weapons are Radio Frequency weapons used for paralysing microwave circuits, computers, radars and other sensors in all communication systems. This is an excellent offensive weapon for cyber warfare which is a warfare in which the Chinese specialise. The PLA has also developed thermo-baric weapons for its artillery and air force. This development has taken place with help from Russia. The PLA is developing hypersonic vehicles like the United States and Russia. These vehicles can also serve as low earth orbit launch vehicles and could be considered as a successor to ICBMs. Considerable effort is being devoted by China in the field of electromagnetic weapons. These weapons use magnets and chemical propellants to give projectiles speed and range far greater than is possible with present-day propellants. Such equipment will enable projectiles to engage targets and counter other projectiles at longer ranges and with high speed.

The Chinese are also focusing on nano-technology to transform the existing equipment in the army. Presently there are more than 100 projects employing around 3000 engineers. The projects include micro weapons, Nano satellites and military equipment. Further, large numbers of projects are dedicated to stealth, counter stealth and biotechnology weapons. Super-cavitating underwater weapons are being procured from Kazakhstan. These move at high speed, often faster than the speed of sound and could be used as torpedoes, anti torpedoes, anti-mines or missiles.

Outer Space

China has since the Korean War, focused on exploration in outer space. The approach of China to outer space has been military-centric from the very beginning. China has remained extremely clear that exploitation of space as the fourth dimension of war is highly important. Effective engagement of targets would need accurate intelligence based on satellite inputs which would lead to correct selection, appropriate corrections during an engagement. Post-Strike Damage Assessment (PDSA) and Command Control Communications Computer Information Intelligence Surveillance Reconnaissance (C^4I^2SR) are major components for command and control of guns, rockets, ships, missiles and submarines. The system depends on inputs provided by satellites deployed in outer space. Satellites of the PLA cover the entire globe, thereby giving it tremendous potential to use platforms in outer space for multifarious purposes. A clear road map for future development exists. Space stations on the lines of the International Space Station are going to be established by 2020. The target vehicle Tiangong-1 was established on September 29, 2011, which can host a crew of three for a limited period. The Tiangong 2 was launched on September 15, 2016. Both these space stations have space for a crew of three. This would be followed by Tiangong 3 and this would be launched in 2020 with the ability to provide 40 days of life support to a crew of three.

Navigation is a major factor in undertaking military operations from the five dimensions of land, sea, air, space and cyber. China has developed the Beidou Satellite System which is similar to the US Global Positioning System (GPS) and the Russian system GLONASS. This is to ensure assured navigational assistance during operations. China launched the Beidou-1A Satellite followed by the Beidou-1B on December 21, 2000, and Beidou-1C on May 25, 2003, thus providing a navigation system comprising three satellites giving locations over China to an accuracy of 10 metres. Over 1000 Beidou-1 terminals were used in the Sichuan earthquake in 2008 for providing information from the earthquake site, and as of date, border guards are equipped with Beidou-1 devices. The global system (Beidou-2) is a new system which in its final shape would have 35 satellites. These would be subdivided into five geostationary orbit satellites for backward compatibility with Beidou-1 and 30 non-geostationary satellites (27 in medium earth orbit and three in inclined geostationary orbit) that will have global coverage. Further free service with 10 metres accuracy is provided commercially for civilian use. The licensed service would be more accurate and utilised for the military purpose. The first satellite of the Beidou-2 was launched on April 13, 2007, and a total of 16 satellites were launched in 2012 and is offering services for the Asia Pacific region. The entire system would be operational by 2020. This would enable China the capability to launch and navigate a weapon precisely to any point on the globe.[17] China is planning the deployment of surveillance devices and thermal lasers which could track and destroy missiles in their boost phase.

Cyber Warfare

China has devoted attention to cyber warfare over the past decade, both in terms of battlefield Information Warfare (IW) and Electronic Warfare (EW). The main doctrine is the 'Integrated Network Electronic Warfare' document which guides PLA computer operations and calls for the combination of network warfare and EW decimation at the start of a conflict to paralyse the C^4I^2SR capabilities of adversaries. The new concept used is 'Information Confrontation' which aims to integrate both electronic and non-electronic aspects of Information Warfare under a single command authority. The PLA views cyber warfare which can be extended to all dimensions during war and peace. Integration of cyber warfare in the PLA has been undertaken by the departments of Information, Strategic Planning and Training. Further, since 2008, all major PLA military exercises, including Kuayue 2009, Shiming Xindong 2010, Lianhe 2011 and recent exercises have significant cyber operations which were both offensive and defensive. The cyber assets of the PLA come under the General Staff Department (GSD). They are controlled by the Electronic Counter Measures (4th Department) and Signals Intelligence (3rd Department). Computer Network Attacks and EW are undertaken by the 4th Department, while the 3rd Department oversees Intelligence Gathering and Computer Network Defence. The Chinese are reported to be associated with numerous cyber-attacks on various networks.

Deng Xiao Ping's vision has transformed China exponentially. Its comprehensive national power has enhanced by an order of magnitude. Militarily, China's defence expenditure is next to the United States and the highest in Asia. With its hard power capabilities and a pragmatic road map, it has become more assertive. Important issues which merit importance are elucidated:

- China has focused a great deal on cyber warfare. An article by Arjun Raf which appeared in www.defencelover.in on January 16, 2018, the issue of cyber espionage by the Third Department of People's Liberation Army. The Third Department of the PLA is responsible for intercepting foreign military communications and producing the necessary intelligence for PLA. They belong to the General Staff Department of the CMC alternatively known as the Technical Reconnaissance Department. They have the biggest signal intelligence network in the Asia Pacific region. The network includes widely spread ground stations, dozens of naval vessels, airborne systems and ground vehicles.

- Several elements of the Third Department were identified by the intelligence services of many countries. They have been involved in numerous cyber-attacks on foreign networks. The Chinese government has declined the same. There are twelve bureaus with specific tasks as stated below:

  - First Bureau (Unit 61786): Located in Northern Beijing. Mission appears to include decryption, encryption and other information security tasks.
  - Second Bureau (Unit 61398): Offices around Shanghai. Specifically targets US and Canada. Emphasizes on political, economic and military intelligence.
  - Third Bureau (Unit 61785): In Southern Beijing. Focuses on collection of line of sight radio communications. This includes border control networks as well as direction finding and emission control.
  - Fourth Bureau (Unit 61419): Around Qingdao. Focused on Japan and South Korea. They have trained linguists to intercept data.
  - Fifth Bureau (Unit 61565): Focused on Russia. Headquartered in Daxing District of Beijing

- Sixth Bureau (Unit 61726): Located In Wachung District of Wuhan. Activity yet be ascertained.
- Seventh Bureau (Unit 61580): North Western District of Beijing. Concentrates on US network models. Engineers specialise in computer network defence and attack.
- Eighth Bureau (Unit 61046): Located in suburbs of North West Beijing. Several trained linguists are employed. Possible focus on Europe and other countries of the globe.
- Ninth Bureau: This is the Department's primary strategic intelligence analysis and data base management bureau. Likely involvement is large scale database management.
- Tenth Bureau (Unit 61886): Located in North West suburbs of Beijing. The main focus is on Russia and Central Asia. Other missions include missile tracking, telemetry and nuclear testing.
- Eleventh Bureau (Unit 61672): Has its Headquarters in Malianwa community of Beijing. Inductions of Russian linguists suggest Russia related missions.
- Twelfth Bureau (Unit 61486): They are located in Shanghai with its Headquarters in Zhabei's district. Involved in satellite communications and space based SIGINT extraction.

The personnel are trained in SIGINT extraction, foreign languages and involved in foreign operations. There are about 20,000 personnel and they are supported by the following institutions:

- Luoyang Institute of Foreign Languages.
- 56th Research Institute with focus in computer technology.
- 57th Research Institute with focus on intercepting communications, signal processing systems and satellite communications.
- 58th Research Institute focused on cryptology and information security technology.

Inputs available are very little and they could be used gainfully in military operations. Several western cyber security firms have identified them as being behind many malware. It is reported that their hackers were behind the ransomware attack which swept the globe. Undoubtedly, China is leaving no stone unturned to optimise its cyber operations to win conflicts.

Smart Power

China has comprehended the term Smart Power coined by Joseph Nye, former Assistant Secretary of Defence, under the Clinton Administration. In international relations, the term Smart Power refers to the combination of Hard Power and Soft Power strategies. The military focus of China is primarily aimed at countering the sole superpower. The strengths developed in attaining this competency can be used to deal with India or any other country.

The PLA promulgated its Political Work Regulations in 2003. The three warfare concept comprises psychological warfare, public opinion warfare and legal warfare. These are written in Chapter 2, Section 18 of the Regulations. Psychological warfare (Xinlizhan). This can occur at the strategic, operational or at the tactical level. According to some analysts, it is at the strategic level that psychological warfare may have the greatest impact, since it may undermine the enemy's will to resist. At the strategic level, psychological warfare is aimed at political and military leaders as also the broader population. Further, it is also aimed at the Chinese population and leaders to enhance the will to fight. Indirectly, it also targets other countries, to encourage them to support China and dissuade them from supporting an opponent. To ensure that psychological warfare creates favourable effects, it will begin prior to formal commencement of open hostilities and will operate in all spheres to include political, military, diplomatic, economic, cultural and religious. It is palpable that this requires time and cannot be done at short notice.

Public opinion warfare (Yulunzhan) refers to the use of media, comprising, internet, television, radio, newspapers and movies to garner public support both at home and abroad for the Chinese position and to create opposition for the adversary. The Chinese accord tremendous credence to shaping the public mind which they refer to as the second battlefield on which depends moral support for operations. This requires tremendous planning and long term efforts. It is obvious that this is an ongoing process requiring intense coordination.

Legal warfare (Faluzhan) is the use of domestic law, the laws of armed conflict and international law in arguing that one's own side is obeying the law and the adversary is violating the law. Further, it also implies justifying Chinese violation of law with strong historical or other reasons. To cite an example, the secession by Taiwan would lead to the violation of the Anti-Secessionist Law passed on March 14, 2005, permitting the PLA to adopt punitive measures. Ultimately the three warfare concept constitutes a form of Smart Warfare, which keeps China vibrant and ready to adopt alternative means to attain their ends. In the Indian context, it would entail the following:

- Sap Indian will and thereby win without fighting;
- Attenuate alliances thereby limiting foreign support;
- Reinforce domestic will.[18]

Keeping the three warfare concept in mind, China would target areas of importance as brought out by the Hong Kong daily Wan Wei Po. As Sun Tzu has stated in 'The Art of War', "The primary objective should be to subjugate other states without actually engaging in armed combat, thereby realising the ideal of complete victory. Whenever possible this should be achieved through diplomatic coercion, thwarting the enemy's plan and alliances as also frustrating his strategy."[19]

China seeks to shape the international environment in accordance with its national interests. In the PLA, the General Political Department (GPD) has a Liaison Department to plan and orchestrate the three warfare concept logically. They function as an interlocking directorate that synchronises relevant party organs, state bureaucracies, military communities, commercial enterprises and informal networks of prominent elites. The GPD is viewing Smart Power in a 20 to 30-year time frame to decide strategic objectives and how they can be applied.

Strategic Application in Future

Land Version

A strategy is a dynamic subject. To visualise strategic application in the future, there is a need to analyse the past and logically deduce application in the future. The Chinese, with their modernisation, have evolved their own method of strategic application. They have a National Defence University, numerous think tanks and military institutions deliberating on national strategy. After Mao's death, Deng Xiao Ping had to wage a grim struggle to liberate China from the Maoist legacy of unending revolution. That legacy lives on, even though internal conditions have changed very dramatically. What it highlights is the basic underlying tensions in the two doctrinal streams of China's strategic culture. The Deng'ist approach is of pragmatic nationalism as opposed to the far more militaristic paradigm of the Seven Military Classics as epitomised by Mao Zedong.

That the battle is still on was highlighted by the recent purge of Bo Xi Lai and the intensive infighting during the transfer of power from the Hu Jintao generation to the fifth generation Xi Jinping. The strain between the two doctrinal strands is now out in the open. After a long period of dormancy, we can now see the PLA's more aggressive approach completely replacing the Dengist Era approach of China's peaceful rise and accommodative strategies. A far more defiant and assertive China is now flexing its muscle against all neighbours not only in the Pacific but also across the land border with the other Asian giant—India. It is pertinent to note that India has a suitable capability to withstand and retaliate.

Mao's China has changed dramatically—so has the strategic culture, which has transformed itself into a far more Westernised avatar while continuing to pay lip service to Maoist doctrines and dogmas of People's War. It is vital that we closely study the remarkable post-1949 doctrinal changes that have transformed organisational structure and equipment, philosophy and profiles of the PLA. We will examine these significant changes and transformations within the PLA.

As per Chinese military writings, post-1949, as China's security situation has changed, the main strategic direction (Zhuyao Zhanlue Fangxiang) has been shifted four times as under:

- **Mid-1950 to Early 1960s:** The main strategic direction faced East against the USA which was then the only power capable of militarily invading China and doing it considerable levels of damage with its nuclear weapons.
- **Mid-1960s to Early 1970s:** The main strategic direction shifted to the North and west against the Soviet Union and remained also poised towards the East as the US threat had not abated and in fact magnified during the Vietnam War. This posed a major strategic dilemma for PLA planners, as doctrinally there can only be one main strategic direction. Mao resolved this with his sudden détente with the USA.

- **Early 1970s to mid-1980s:** The main strategic direction now became fixed to the North primarily against the Soviet Union. The Soviet Union was the only power that could have credibly carried out a major land invasion of China in concert with the use of tactical nuclear weapons. The Soviet invasions of Czechoslovakia and Afghanistan had added to Chinese paranoia about a Soviet threat and social imperialism.
- **Mid-1980s to early 1990s:** As the Chinese economy grew by leaps and bounds, the coastal economic zones became the powerhouse of not just the Chinese, but also the global economy. These now emerged increasingly as a major vulnerability that had to be defended. With the economic collapse of the USSR, there was no longer any credible threat of a major land invasion of China. The main strategic direction now shifted to a coastal concept with no specific enemy defined. PLA thinking graduated to the era of local wars and the operational focus in the initial stages was mostly on Taiwan.

It is pertinent to note that Marshal Peng De Huai was one China's ablest and professional combat leaders. His experience in the Korean War had convinced him of the need to rapidly modernise the PLA. The PLA had managed to do so well against far more modern armies simply by virtue of its much greater combat experience and battle-hardened military leadership and rank and file. Peng, the moderniser, however, was purged by Mao Zedong in 1959 just six years after the Korean War. Mao and Lin Biao clung on tenaciously to their Peoples War experience. Mao's Great Leap Forward and then the most disastrous Cultural Revolution greatly delayed the military modernisation of China. It was only after Lin Biao's failed coup and Mao's demise in 1975, that Deng Xiao Peng could assume charge in China. This epitomised the fierce struggle between the modern nationalist paradigm and the Maoist paradigm of ceaseless war and continuing revolution. Mao's emphasis on human resources over weapons and material factors historically delayed the modernisation of the Chinese military.

Deng and his supporters had carefully studied the rise and fall of the Nazis in Germany. They realised that without significant economic modernisation, no military modernisation was possible. The massive casualties suffered in the costly war in 1979 against Vietnam, convinced Deng of the imperative need for Chinese military modernisation. Thus Deng began the

Four Modernisations of China. Once again we see the Chinese civilisational genius for long term perspective thinking. Deng consciously decided that China needed a period of peace to complete its economic, scientific and military modernisations. The breakup of the Soviet Union removed the only credible and the somewhat real threat of a massive land invasion of China. Some of the seminal events that drove doctrinal evolution in the PLA can thus be listed as:

- The Korean War 1950-53;
- Stoppage of Soviet assistance 1959;
- The 1962 War with India;
- The 1969 Border War with USSR;
- The 1979 Border War with Vietnam;
- The1989 Tiananmen square massacre and embargo of Western military supplies;
- The shock of the 1991 Gulf War. This really shook the Chinese;
- The US decision to send two Carrier Battle Groups at the peak of the Taiwan Crisis in 1995-96.

Each of these seminal events had a major impact on the doctrinal evolution of the PLA. It is essential to summarise the major military doctrinal changes that occurred as a result of these drivers. Paul B Godwin writes of these changes in the Chinese Military Doctrine. He states that the enduring requirement to defeat materially superior opponents explains trenchant Chinese adherence to Maoist theories developed in the 1920s and 1930s during the prolonged civil war and later during Japan's military invasion. Further, great emphasis was placed on offensive operations conducted with speed and lethality. Active defence was the main doctrine of the Chinese Civil War and the primary basis of Mao's attempts to retain the initiative at all times—even in the conduct of the strategically defensive campaign

The essence of Mao's response to his forces' inferiority in arms, equipment and training was to conduct a protracted war (Chi Jiu Zhan) of attrition while preparing for the time when the asymmetry between the Communist Forces and its enemies would be overcome. Hence, the major Chinese emphasis on the Peoples' War (or Renmin Zhanzhen). A core doctrinal principle was "Active Defence" or defence through active engagement. Mao exhorted his forces to conduct offensive operations within the constraints of a defensive strategy. Without this doctrinal underpinning, Mao feared that a protracted war would become bogged down in passive defence (Xiaji Fangu). This would lead to a loss of initiative and a reactive stance that could have seriously eroded morale and sapped the will to fight protracted wars. Even though at the strategic level, he was forced to go on the defensive, at the operational and tactical level, he sought quick engagements to annihilate the enemy. Battles cannot be protracted because extended engagements are costly in both men and weapons. However, to wear down a superior enemy, the war had to be extended in time and space. The intensity of the civil war can be gauged from the fact that by the time of the Long March and the retreat of the PLA to North and Central China in 1934-35, Mao and the PLA were down to just 10,000 men. Amazingly by 1949, these had grown to five field armies numbering four million.

Post-1949, the important doctrinal changes in the PLA, therefore, occurred as a result of the experience in the Korean War. There was a change from the Peoples' War to Peoples' War under Modern Conditions. Attritional and material modernisation (that Marshal Peng De Huai wanted after the Korean War) however was badly delayed by the Great Leap Forward and then the chaos and turbulence of the Great Cultural Revolution. Peng himself was sacked in1959. It was Gen Su Yu who wrote his famous article introducing the term Peoples' War under Modern Conditions. By 1971, the USSR had emerged as the most serious threat and the strategic alliance with the USA was used to counter it. By 1990, the Soviet Union had collapsed. The USA and the USSR had been the only military powers which could have actually invaded China. Of these, the Soviet Union was a far more credible threat as it had the resources to undertake a fairly credible land invasion of China. With the breakup of the USSR, this threat of a large scale invasion receded dramatically. China's paramount leader Deng Xiao Peng, therefore, came to the clear cut determination that massive conventional wars and invasion of China (as per the First and Second World War models) were no longer possible. There was, therefore, the very deliberate shift from large scale wars to limited or local wars and then as the first Gulf War happened, to local wars under hi-tech conditions. After Gulf War II, they became local wars under conditions of information. The doctrinal progression can, therefore, be summed up as given in the Figure 3.3 below:

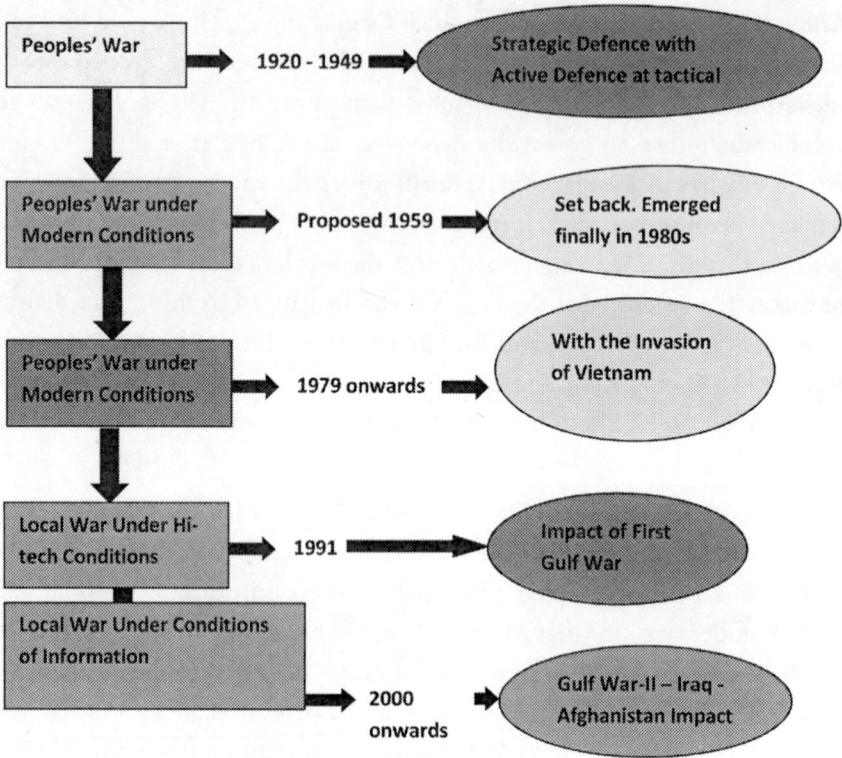

Figure 3.3: Warfare Progression as Deduced in the Book

The changing technology of war and China's own dramatically altered power profile made the classical Peoples' War an idea of the past. With such unprecedented economic development and industrialisation, it became impossible for China to accept major loss of territory or organise such defence in depth and protraction or mass mobilisation. Wars henceforth would be short, swift, limited and localised. The 1979 Sino-Vietnam War epitomised such conflicts. These called for rapid mobilisation, defence of the periphery and, therefore, the need for very rapid military modernisation.[20] Active Defence or Strategic Defence with Tactical Offensive (Jyi Fangyu) has always been one of the constant themes in Chinese strategic debates. It has, however, continued to be accorded ever newer interpretations and connotations. It has virtually been set up as an independent paradigm in itself. It has undergone a transition from war prevention to war fighting as also from protracted, total war to swift and limited war operations. This has been the overall trend in China's war fighting doctrines in the last 50 years.

Naval Version

China has always been a traditional conventional and land-centric power. Its huge mass armies have had excellent tactical mobility on foot. Its strategic mobility, however, was confined to the rail network of China. Deng Xiao Peng had seen the collapse of the Soviet Union and the failure of the Socialist Model of centralised planning. He began by dismantling the Agricultural Communes and giving small plots of land to Chinese peasants. This privatisation produced an Agricultural Revolution of self-sufficiency in food grains and vegetables. Based upon this he began to industrialise China in a major way. With American and Western involvement and hand me down technologies, he soon made China the workshop of the world for cheap, low-end manufacture. By the controlled price of the Chinese currency (Yuan), China made its exports highly competitive. It was emulating the Japanese export or perish model of cheap manufacture and keeping the value of its currency artificially depressed to make its exports competitive.

Deng and his Defence Minister Ma Xiaotian had studied the rise and fall of Nazi Germany and the Soviet Union and learnt their lessons. Economic modernisation, they were convinced, had to precede military modernisation. That was the cardinal error Germany had made during World War II. It militarised and launched a war well before it had consolidated economically. The coastal region became the economic powerhouse of China and then the world. The Special Economic Zones (SEZs) of Shanghai and Guangdong flourished even as the interior provinces remained impoverished. The coastal belt was the basis of the Chinese economic miracle and the region. Its economic powerhouse had now to be strongly defended from attacks, invasions, attrition by air attacks, cruise missile strikes and blockades. Trading space for time in such areas was now simply out of question.

China's economy grew by leaps and bounds. China's GDP grew at almost 10 per cent per annum for almost two decades in the 1990s and the first decade of the 21st century. China's new production centres on the coast are now vulnerable and exposed to attacks from the sea flank. The east coast area of Shanghai and Guangdong is the new economic powerhouse of China and indeed of the Asia Pacific Rim. This is the new core area of vulnerability, and hence, is the new criticality that China has to defend at all costs. It is this that has caused a paradigm shift in Chinas military orientation from a continental to a maritime outlook and the Chinese Navy has acquired a new centrality in Chinese thinking. Trends in contemporary conflict clearly favour a hi-tech and limited war. The emphasis, therefore, has shifted towards positional and forward defence and offensive. The Maoist Peoples' War concepts of protraction of the war and strategic retreat to lure the enemy deep into Chinese territory are no longer viable propositions as the value of Chinese industrial real estate has risen exponentially. China's entire commerce is largely carried by sea. By 1993 China had become a net importer of energy. The industrialisation of China rapidly increased its demand for oil and gas, which is now escalating at an exponential rate as the economy grows. China today is the largest consumer of petroleum in the world. Most of this comes from the Middle East, the Persian Gulf and North Africa by sea and has to pass through choke points of the Malacca Straits. China now has to defend its sea lines of communication.

The intense hunger for energy resources has compelled China to secure the South China Sea Basin where it has anticipated the existence of huge reserves of oil and natural gas. This has directly brought it into conflict with the other littoral states with competing claims on the South China Sea. This included the South East Asian states of Vietnam, Indonesia and The Philippines. The dispute over the Senkaku Islands had the potential to bring it into conflict with Japan. Besides, China's main combat target was Taiwan and the threat to unify this "renegade province" by military force implied the ability to mount a major amphibious invasion and prevent the United States from intervening in any such conflict.

All this led to a gradual shift in orientation from the land-based PLA to an increasing emphasis on Chinese Navy (PLAN). personalities playing a role in such power shifts. The Chinese Admiral Liu Huaquing was the PLAN Chief from 1982 to 1988. He was very close to Deng Xiao Peng. He went on to become the Vice Chairman of the Central Military Commission (CMC), from which high ranking post, he was in a strong position to oversee the growth and modernisation of the PLAN. The significant rise in the power and reach of the Chinese Navy and its growing centrality in the PRC's security concern can largely be attributed to this Chinese Mahan. It was Admiral Liu Huaquing who shaped the evolution of Chinese Naval Doctrine and Naval Strategy from mere coastal defence to sea-ward defence (off-shore defence) based on the First and second Chain of Islands and then towards a full-fledged

Blue Water capability. Huaquing stressed on the need for sea control between the Chinese coast and the first chain of islands stretching from the Kuriles, Japan, Reylain, Taiwan and The Philippines.

In defining the chains of islands, Admiral Liu Huaquing was transferring the traditional Chinese Great Wall, land-mindset to the sea. Except that instead of coastal or peripheral defence, he was trying to add depth and cushion space to the vital Chinese economic heartland of coastal cities and provinces. As rhetoric over Taiwan intensified, and China unleashed its coercive military strategy of large scale exercises and rocket firings over Taiwan, the US responded in 1995-96 by dispatching two Carrier Battle Groups (CBGs) and Cruise Missiles mounted on its cruisers and destroyers. The Chinese Navy was shaken by this assertive projection of US naval power and thereafter resolved that they would find an antidote to the threat posed by CBGs and cruise missiles. This triggered the quest for aircraft carrier killer missiles like the Dong Feng 21D that would put into effect an Anti-Access/Area Denial Strategy against the United States. This needed not just be ballistic missiles that could hit a CBG some two to three thousand km out at sea, but also enhance satellite surveillance capability to pick up these US warships thousands of km from the Chinese shoreline. It also called for packs of nuclear and diesel-electric submarines that would tag and attack these advancing naval CBGs in droves. These attacks would start not on the first chain of islands but now, as Huaquing proposed, from the second chain of islands itself. Huaquing propounded the need for pushing Chinese Naval defences out to the Second Chain of Islands (formed by the Bonim, the Mariana, Guam and the Carolene).[21]

This change from a coastal defence strategy (Jinhai Fangyu) to offshore defence (Jenyang Fangyu) would extend the Chinese naval perimeter out to 200-400 nautical miles from the Chinese coastline and even more in the case of the South China Sea. Admiral Huaquing drew up a long term perspective plan to graduate from a Brown Water Coastal Navy to one that would reach out to the First and Second Chain of Islands and then transit to a full-fledged Blue Water Navy (Yuanjong Haijung) by 2050. In pursuit of this capability, the Chinese Navy has operationalised the ex-Soviet aircraft carrier Varyag; is building two more and has also unleashed a major shipbuilding programme to build Luda and Luhu class missile destroyers, Jiangyu and Jiangwu class frigates and Han class nuclear submarines. To enhance sea denial capabilities, it also went in for 12 Russian Kilo class diesel electric submarines and acquired the SU-27 and SU-30 Soviet aircraft to extend its reach out to the sea. By 2009, the Chinese had developed the Dong Feng 21D aircraft carrier killer missiles along with its associated surveillance satellites to pick up and track US aircraft carriers. This seems to have been a psychological watershed of sorts. With this capability actualised, the Chinese felt they had the answer to the American CBGs. From 2009 onwards, we see the sudden onset of a very aggressive and defiant phase in Chinese attitude in international relations.

Air Power Strategy

General Xu Quiliang, the former head of the PLAAF, and General Liu Yazhou (formerly Political Commissioner of the National Defence University (NDU)), are the army officers who evolved Chinese Air Force strategy. General Liu Yazhou is an acknowledged Chinese thinker on air power and has constantly been writing on how to learn from the American employment of airpower and apply it in the Chinese context. Incidentally, he also has been writing on the need for democratising the Chinese political process. He was one of the first PLAAF officers to be appointed Deputy Chief of the General Staff. This underlines the major effort that China is making to modernise and upgrade its air force. From a fleet of vintage Soviet-era jets of the second and third generation like MiG-17, MiG-19 and MiG-21 and its variants, it is now a modern air force with Fourth Generation fighters like the Soviet SU-27 and SU-30; and the copies of SU-27 (J-11) as also the Israeli Lavi (equivalent to the American F-16) or the J-10 fighter. Cheaper variants of this—the JF-17—have been jointly produced with Pakistan.

Figure 3.4: Chinese J-10 Fighter[22]

The greatest achievement of China was the unveiling of two Fifth Generation Stealth Fighter prototypes—the J-20 (the equivalent of the USA's F-22 Raptor) and the J-31 (the equivalent of US Naval version of the Lightning

Stealth Fighter F-35). China already has AWACs and air-to-air refuelling fleets. By 2020, it will have some 1,300 4th Generation fighters, and then, perhaps the first batch of Fifth Generation fighters would be operational. Airpower is the key to victory over land or sea environments and it is the growth of Chinese airpower that should be of the most critical concern to adversaries and very specifically to India. Aerospace power is the logical extension of airpower.

Figure 3.5: Chinese J-20 Fifth Generation Fighter Aircraft[23]

Even in this field, the Chinese have made path-breaking strides. By 2030, China will have over 100 surveillance satellites and its own Navigation Systems. Besides, it has already demonstrated the ability to shoot down enemy satellites in low earth orbit. It has conducted many manned space flights and is in the process of building its own space station. Coupled with a radical increase in Chinese capabilities for cyber warfare, we see a drive for dominance in outer space, the electromagnetic spectrum as also in the cyberspace.

Aspects regarding Doctrinal Changes

The Peoples' War Doctrine was premised upon the fundamental core of a weak military force pitched against a far stronger one. It was hence relevant to the era of the Chinese Civil War (the 1920s and 1930s), as also the period of the Chinese invasion by Japan. As a strong Communist state consolidated its hold over the whole of China, as China has grown in economic and military power and developmental terms, the entire discourse on which the Peoples' War Doctrine was premised, has become totally outdated and irrelevant. With such massive economic development in China's coastal zones and cities, trading space for time and permitting deep strategic penetrations to lure the enemy in deep and destroy him, has become untenable. This could have be done when China was a highly underdeveloped and poor country with even its agriculture confined to certain areas. The hilly and rugged Chinese terrain was value-neutral, and in the battle with a far stronger industrial adversary, such value-neutral space could be easily traded for time. It was like a naval battle where the sea space has no inherent value. It is merely the medium of manoeuvre. Chinese real estate is no longer value neutral. The new coastal wealth production centres are critical to the Chinese economy. This central construct of Mao's People's War Doctrine is now untenable. The first epoch of challenge to Peoples' War Doctrine came immediately after the Korean War when Marshal Peng De Huai had first asked for rapid military modernisation.

By 1959, the Peoples' War under Modern Conditions was already being talked of openly. It is just that Mao and his followers had invested too much emotional capital in this concept and as long as powerful adversaries like the United States of America and Soviet Union were inimical, it still held a lot of relevance to these elites as a means of deterrence and strategic communication. One can occupy the whole of China but one cannot subdue it—the cost of which would be unthinkable. Thus US defence intelligence agencies have defined the Peoples' War as, "A doctrine for the defence of China against various types of wars, ranging from a surprise long-range nuclear strike combined with a massive ground invasion, to a ground attack with limited objectives. It is premised upon the participation of the whole population and mobilisation of all the country's reserves for as long as it takes to defeat any invader. This doctrine was meant to assure both the Chinese people and any potential invader, that in case of war, there will be no surrender, no collaboration and even if China's conventional forces are defeated, unremitting resistance will continue till the invader withdraws."

This was primarily a deterrent message to potential invaders. The threat of a US invasion declined dramatically after the Vietnam War. The more serious threat now was the Soviet Union. To counter it, Mao aligned with the USA. By 1990, even the Soviet Union had collapsed and with that, the last credible threat of massive invasion receded totally. The Peoples' War Doctrine was now genuinely redundant. In doctrinal terms, therefore, by the early 1980s itself, there was a fundamental shift of emphasis from not just defending but also to winning wars.

In fact, in January 1985, a historic resolution was passed in the enlarged Central Military Commission (CMC) meeting—called "Strategic Challenge in Guiding Thoughts on National Defence". As per Admiral Liu Huaquing, this strategy was clearly aimed at working an operational doctrine, as also the technological wherewithal for building Active Defence beyond China's territorial area. Party Gen Secretary Zhao Zhyang emphasised Active Defence again in 1988 by introducing the "Strategy of Offshore Defence". The debate, he stressed, focused on two fundamental issues:

- What should be the goal of the New Security Strategy?
- What kind of military forces should China have to carry out the New Strategy?

Broadly by this time, the Chinese strategic establishment had come to the clear cut determination that of the three kinds of wars that China could face viz. World War or a General Global Conflict; Large scale invasion/aggression by a foreign country and Limited War or a Border Conflict—only the last named could be expected to really happen. China has embarked upon a long term plan to prepare itself for such contingencies. It has carefully integrated long term objectives with capital-intensive, hi-tech military modernisation.[24]

In effect, therefore, the active defence aspect of the Peoples' War under Modern Conditions has introduced five significant deviations from Active Defence in Mao's Peoples War concept. These are:

- Rather than luring the enemy in deep, the adversary has to be defeated close to the borders.
- Early battles rather than late battles were considered decisive.
- The new concept seemed to completely reject the notion of a Peoples' War.
- Positional War was stressed as much as Mao's mobile wars and fluid front.
- Cities were now to be defended as opposed to the earlier Maoist dictums of vacating the cities to retreat to the vast rural areas from where the enemy could be surrounded and annihilated.

Active Defence is now being strengthened through the screws of prediction, preemption and coercion. These are now an integral part of China's new war fighting doctrine of Limited/Local Wars under Hi-Tech Conditions.

Types of Limited War

Paul H Godwin carried out detailed studies on the Chinese concept of Limited War and characterised the five basic types of limited conflicts that could occur:

- Small scale conflicts restricted to contested border territories;
- Conflicts over territorial seas and islands;
- Surprise air attacks;
- Defence against deliberately limited attacks into Chinese territory.
- Punitive counterattacks launched by China into enemy territory to oppose the invasion, protect sovereignty or to uphold justice or dispel threats.[25]

In actual fact, it is the last named contingency that we are most likely to see in the future. The "Hifazhiren"—Chinese concept of striking only after the enemy has struck and thereby claiming the Chinese war to be just and virtuous, now seems to have been substantially modified. During the Gulf War I, the Chinese watched with consternation as Saddam Hussein sat back passively and let the Americans methodically build up huge force levels for the attack. The Chinese are quite clear that such a buildup of hostile forces represents a threat to Chinese sovereignty and national security, and preemption in such cases is fully justified. The enemy has already taken the first step by mobilising his forces and China can now react pre-emptively. The entire emphasis is on retaining the initiative to commence and terminate the conflict on Chinese terms. This Active Defence methodology, therefore, envisages not a defensive counter-attack but rather a pre-emptive attack.

The pre-emptive could well entail an attack on enemy satellites coupled with cyber-attacks and a barrage of conventional tipped and cruise missiles on key airfields and command, control and communication nodes. It is quite possible that these attacks could be denied. China now has over 1,200 conventional tipped short-range ballistic missiles, which it will fire to overwhelm the attacker even before the enemy has launched his first strike. The current versatile technological innovation has been the Dong Feng 21D Anti-Ship Ballistic Missile that can attack and sink such advancing Aircraft Carrier Battle Groups about 1800 kilometres out to sea. These can thus be destroyed well before they can launch their attack aircraft or cruise missiles on Chinese shore-based targets. The Chinese have launched a constellation of three Naval Surveillance Satellites to pick up US Aircraft Carrier Battle Groups

(CBGs) as they move towards China. The satellites would also pick up their communication and electronic signatures and target them well before they could even think of launching their attack aircraft or cruise missiles. The entire Chinese Anti-Access or Area Denial Strategy hinges on this kind of a preemptive attack well away from the Chinese shores.

The Dong Feng 21D missiles, therefore, could well turn out to be a significant game-changer in naval warfare and make the CBG a less potent force. Not only the Dong Fengs'—Chinese nuclear and conventional submarines will hurl themselves against these advancing CBGs in droves. Once they are in range, the PLAAF's and PLAN's SU-27 and SU-30s and J-11 fighters would hurl themselves at whatever remains of these CBGs. The Dong Feng 21D has so far not been tested in combat. But the PLAN seems supremely convinced that it has a battle winning factor up its sleeve that can effectively deter the US from intervening in any conflict in the Asia-Pacific. It is perhaps this conviction that has perhaps seen a sea change in the Chinese attitude since 2009. By 2010-11, this defiance had acquired the contours of a reckless assertion and aggression against all comers—starting from Japan to Vietnam, Philippines and Indonesia and barely concealed threats against the USA. Not just at sea—Chinese aggression is equally evident on land on its disputed borders with India and is now trying to hem in India with its String of Pearls strategy in the Indian Ocean Region (IOR). All these Chinese moves are so characteristic of the Chinese game of Weiqi, which seeks to strategically encircle the adversary.

China would possibly undertake conflicts with limited political objectives and geographic scope short in duration, but decisive in strategic outcomes. They are usually fought over territorial claims, economic disputes, or ethnic rivalries. These wars are not region-wide, much less global conflicts but they can be very large in scale and intensity. These then are the types of wars that China is now preparing to fight.[26]

War Zone Campaigning

War Zone campaigning is designed to aid in the conduct of limited wars. It stresses on the modernisation of the armed-forces in order to create "Pockets of Excellence". These have been established in terms of two massive Rapid Reaction Forces (or to use the exact Chinese phraseology—Resolving

Emergency Mobile Combat Forces—REMCFs). These are selectively assembled, advanced capabilities that are supposed to offset the enemies' technological advantage in a military conflict. It also refers to trans-regional mobility—the ability to focus resources from diverse military regions (now Theatre Commands) onto one chosen war zone where decisive results are aimed at in a limited war of short duration but of very high intensity. Under war Zone Campaigning, the military command chain would change into the designated War Zone representative who would be directly responsible to the CMC. Thus in a conflict with India, the War Zone headquarters would be set up in Lhasa and bring under its control not only the forces and logistical support elements of the Chengdu and Lanzhou Military Area Commands (newly formed Western Theatre Command) but also the 15 AB Corps and any other RRFs inducted from the other military regions of China for a decisive battle in a limited war context. China has massively downsized its huge infantry—predominant Army from some four million men to just 1.6 million. However, this quantitative downsizing has been compensated for by extensive modernisation of the ground force in terms of mechanisation and digitisation. The mechanisation process is virtually complete and the digitisation is proceeding steadily.

Assassins Mace

This term was used to describe the entirety of weapons systems strategic and tactical that are specifically used to exploit an enemy's weakness (comprehensive notion of a weapon system and tactics). The DF-21D Anti-Ship ballistic missile is just such a combination of a weapons system and tactics designed to defeat or deter intervention by US CBGs in any conflict involving China.

The chances of miscalculation and inadvertent and sudden escalation are immense and dangerous. Asia is witness to the largest regional arms buildup since the World War II. Militant nationalism is on the rise in most Asian countries. In China, it is being most deliberately stoked by the current President Xi Jinping. This has triggered a chain reaction in Japan, Vietnam, Philippines, Thailand and Indonesia. Despite the overtly peaceful orientation of the current Indian administration, there are clear stirrings of nationalism even in India—where such border issues have now entered the discourse of domestic politics and the media would not let the government bend beyond a point. The current government in India has strengthened India's foreign policy and tried to diplomatically have good relations with China as observed at the Wuhan Summit held on April 27 and 28, 2018.

The chances of accidental conflicts and local wars erupting in Asia are increasing by the day. India is particularly vulnerable because the Chinese in the Korean War had always selected the weaker South Korean formations for attack and destruction. Simply due to its inordinately slow arms build-up— India remains the most vulnerable of all major adversaries in Asia—at least till 2020. Unless the Indian government speeds up its arms acquisition drive, it could invite a preemptive attack to stall its military and infrastructure buildup— that will ensure that China is not engaged in a two-front war.

Future Shape of PLA

Xi Jinping, the current President and the Chairman of the Central Military Commission (CMC) and General Secretary of the CCP, is slated to occupy these positions for life. He has often spoken of the Chinese Dream which primarily comprises Strength and Wealth.[27] The PLA is being strengthened and in another decade would possibly be the most powerful armed forces, second only to the United States. While we have analysed the modernisation and strategic culture, it would be essential to examine the future shape of the PLA.

To begin let us examine the command and control structure from what it was and the changes it needs for the future. Generically the PLA includes the PLA Ground Forces, the PLA Navy (PLAN), PLA Air Force (PLAAF) and the 2nd Artillery Corps—which is its Strategic Nuclear Force. The Chinese armed forces are under the leadership of the CCP. This leadership is exercised through the Central Military Commission (CMC).[27] There two Military Commissions—one for the party and the other one for the state:

- The Central Military Commission of the CCP.
- Central Military Commission of the PRC.

In fact, these are almost identical. Both commissions have the same membership structure. The most important distinction is the existence of a General Office in the Party CMC. The General Office facilitates and manages interaction amongst China's most senior military leaders. Security policies are shaped by these groups within the Central Committee of the CPC:

- Leading Small Group on Taiwan Affairs;
- Leading Small Group on Foreign Affairs;
- Leading Small Group on National Security. This was established in 2001. This is the Crisis Management Group that coordinates security Policies between the PLA and Foreign Ministry and other agencies.

It is pertinent to note that the party controls the PLA and often the Chinese Government is unaware of detailed actions undertaken by the PLA as minute issues are discussed at the CMC of the party.

The National People's Congress (NPC) decides on war and peace; issues proclamations of a state of war and decides on general or political mobilisation. In practice this rarely came into play as conflicts were limited in nature and scope, and required no general declaration of war.

The State Council directs and administers National Defence including:

- Making National Defence Development plans;
- Formulating principles;
- The mobilisation of the national economy and armed forces;
- National Defence education;

The Ministry of National Defence comes under the State Council. The CMC decides the:

- Military strategy and guidelines for armed forces;
- Administers the building of the PLA;
- Submits proposals related to National Defence.

During the Maoist Era—the civilian leadership held senior military positions and directed campaigns. Hence the role of Mao and his generals in the CMC was overwhelming and overriding till the end of the Maoist Era. Deng Xiao Ping was the last of the Long Marchers and the stamp of his leadership was decisive and clearly visible in the war against Vietnam in 1979. However, with the arrival of the post-Mao civilian leadership of technocrats and party apparatchiks, it is to be seen how the higher command and control arrangement will function in practice. The role of the president is likely to be overwhelming and detailed control of limited wars will perforce be exercised through the CMC. In the present case, President Xi Jinping is holding all three positions, i.e., Chairman of the Party, Head of the executive and Head of the CMC. He would ensure that the PLA becomes a modernised force by 2030. As a matter of fact, he made it his primary task to get to know the senior PLA leadership even before he officially took charge.

Xi Jinping has also ensured obedience by putting in place "princelings" and loyalists in key appointments, who would faithfully carry out his directions. He started this well before he formally occupied the post. This, in turn, incited his PLA commanders to act assertively militarily to impress their new boss and gain his favour as leaders who would deliver in times of war or conflict. There were sudden bouts of aggression against Japan and the South Eastern Asian neighbours in the South China Sea. Thus in 2009, the world was surprised by an uncharacteristic burst of aggression from the PLA against all of China's neighbours over land or maritime boundary disputes. After years of the Dengist, low-profile policy of "hide your capabilities, bide your time", the PLA suddenly turned aggressive. What is quite evident now is the way PLA generals are clearly asserting themselves against the foreign ministry and other civilian policy-making organs of the state since 2009. There is speculation that the generals are trying to prove themselves to "new boss" Xi Jinping as he goes about touring the Military Regions (MRs) to get to know his military leadership and identify those he thinks can deliver. The Chinese have by and large identified their new strategic direction as being the defence of coastal cities and economic engines of production along the east coast.

In all future conflicts, the CMC will be the primary command and control organ of state. As per current military reforms, the CMC would have a modified organisation by 2020. While the reform process is taking place, it would be essential to understand the erstwhile constitution of the CMC from the point of view of its past functioning. The CMC has the following under its wings:

- PLA General Staff HQ;
- PLA Political Department;
- General Logistics Department;
- General Armament Department.

As stated, in the Maoist Era, the CMC was the primary command authority. There was a great deal of coordination and synthesis as the civilian leadership was former senior PLA commanders, each with considerable hands-on military experience. Hence the CMC even coordinated media themes of information warfare and public posturing. The current reforms undertaken in February

2016 have made the CMC a more important player in Chinese defence planning and execution.

The 1962 war with India was totally controlled and directed by Mao and the CMC. Deng Xiao Ping followed a similar path. He enforced his ultimate control over the PLA by handpicking appointments for top slots. Before taking over, Deng had extensively toured his military formations and put in place commanders he had served with and trusted. He then deliberately unleashed a war on Vietnam not only to test his army, but also to unify the PLA and the country solidly behind him. Xi Jinping has followed the same methodology, energising and testing his military leadership before assuming charge. The PLA also asserted itself vis-à-vis the Pacific. The Chinese Foreign Ministry had so far, pushed the Dengist agenda of seeking a peaceful periphery, hiding their abilities and biding their time.

Currently, the CMC is being reformed. It would eventually have seven departments, three commissions and five offices. The seven departments would be the General Office, Joint Staff, Political Work, Logistic Support, Equipment Development and National Mobilisation. The three commissions would be Discipline & Inspection, Political & Legal Affairs and Science & Technology. The five offices would be Strategic Planning, Reform & Organisational Structure, International Military Cooperation, Audit Bureau and Office Administration. This reorganisation is to be completed by 2020.

It would take a few more years to stabilise these military institutions. Accordingly, the charter of the various components of the erstwhile CMC is described below. Though changes have been undertaken by Xi Jinping, it is important to understand the details given below.

PLA General Staff HQ

- Organises and directs the development of China's armed forces and organises and commands their military operations
- Has departments for operations, intelligence, communications, military training and arms, adjutant and force structures, mobilisation, electronic countermeasures, army aviation, foreign affairs etc.
- Its main functions and powers are to put forward proposals on major issues of military building and operations; organise and exercise strategic command; organise and direct war preparations as well as military training and mobilization.

Strategic Planning Department

In November 2011, the PLA Daily website announced the formation of a new Strategic Planning Department-under the General Staff Department. This was charged with studying critical strategic issues, drafting plans and reform proposals for PLA development, submitting suggestions on the allocation of resources to PLA, and strategic resources. Many senior PLA officers felt the strategic planning centre would become an authoritative and comprehensive planning centre. It was established due to developments in the South China Sea, which had caught the PLA by surprise. The PLA felt it had lost the initiative at home and abroad and that China was not behaving like a great power. The PLA appears to be faulting the party and the government for being soft to challenges. The PLA is clearly trying to assert itself on security issues. Hu Jin Tao had handed over the responsibilities of psychological operations, media operations, and legal warfare to the PLA. These had earlier been handled by the CCP's propaganda department. The PLA has now usurped these functions under the three warfare's strategy.

General Political Department

- Administers and organises the armed forces party and political work;
- It has departments for party affairs, personnel, publicity, security, discipline, inspection and civil-military affairs;
- It ensures the armed forces compliance with implementation of the principles and policies of the party and provides guidance on political work.

General Logistical Department

- This administers the logistical work of the armed forces departments;
- It deals with overall planning and equipment for all arms and services;
- It deals with all financial matters, capital construction and barracks, Quarter Master materials, fuel oil & lubricants (FOL), auditing, health administration, military transport and conducts all military procurement.

General Armament Department (GAD)

- Its charter is the provision of equipment for the armed forces;
- It carries out overall planning for equipment for all arms and services;
- Procures the army's military equipment, research & development (R&D);

- General purpose equipment support;
- Electronic, information infrastructure;
- Formulates strategic programs, plans and policies and makes rules and regulations for equipment development;
- Organises equipment R&D, experimentation, procurement, combat service, maintenance and support;
- Administers PLA funds for equipment build up.

The CMC also oversees the Commissions of Science, Technology, Industry and National Defense (COSTIND). This was earlier looking after R&D but the same has been transferred to the GAD department under the CMC. Apart from the CMC other important security structures are elucidated below. The CMC under reform will incorporate all aspects in the erstwhile CMC. The emphasis in the new CMC will be on coordination and jointness. Further, the CMC becomes the General Headquarters for the PLA.

The Ministry for State Security: It conducts domestic and foreign intelligence. The militia and PAP units will reinforce the PLA in any contingency on Chinese territory.

Internal Security

Internal Security responsibility falls on the Ministry for Public Security. It has:

- 1.7 million police personnel;
- 1.3 million People's Armed Police (PAP), most of whom have been demobilised from the PLA itself;
- The several million strong (10 million strong?) militia forces.

People's Armed Police (PAP): The PAP comes under the command of the CMC and State Council. Internal Security Force serves as light infantry during any war on Chinese soil. Some PAP units are responsible for border security and guarding critical infrastructure

Structure of the PLA Ground Forces

The PLA ground forces are currently divided into seven Military Area Commands (MAC). As per the latest reforms, they are being reorganised into five theatre commands. This process is likely to be completed by 2020. Even before there was an ongoing debate on whether these must be further reduced to Five instead of seven MRs. The PLA ground forces maintain a two-tier classification:

- **Class A Units:** Maintain personnel and material in combat readiness at all times.
- **Class B Units:** These need more time to reach full operational status.

As stated, the PLA ground forces are divided into MACs. The PLA Navy (PLAN) in turn is organised into Fleet Commands (The Fleet Commander serves as the Deputy MR Commander). The PLA Air Force (PLAAF) is divided into MR Air Commands. The PLA ground forces are currently divided into 18 group armies.

Former Military Area Commands (MACs) (Now being reorganised as Joint Theatre Commands)

These have the headquarters of the political department, the joint logistics department and the armament department. The MAC would generally have two or more combined army corps, logistics support units along with provincial military commands (that are responsible for reserve force building; peacetime enlistment and wartime strength mobilisation) and the units of the various branches. The MACs are now designed to conduct joint theatre operations in five joint theatre commands. These seven MACs are the Shenyang, Beijing, Lanzhou, Jinan, Nanjing, Guangzhou and Chengdu. As stated, the ongoing debate is whether these should be reduced to five. In the event of being reduced to five, Lanzhou would include Chengdu MR and Beijing would include the Shenyang MAC. Presently there is an Air Command in each of the seven MACs. The five theatre commands being formed, would include elements of the navy and the air force. These five theatre commands are North, West, South, East and Central. The Northern is based toward Russia, West to India, South to Vietnam & the South China Sea, East to Taiwan, Central is in conjunction with East to Korea and Japan.

Group Armies

These are corps-sized formations, which generally consist of three divisions and support units. A Standard Group Army would consist of three infantry divisions, one artillery division, one tank brigade, one aviation, one engineer and one recce regiment. The average number of troops may decline as the divisions are being gradually replaced with brigades. Based on the US pattern, these may all be organised on a corps-brigade-battalion chain of command. The Chinese attempt to ape the US model more suited for expeditionary warfare indicates the Chinese drift towards theoretical formulations without testing them in combat conditions. In intense air-ground engagements, the loss of divisional level of command element is likely to place overload on the sole corps level headquarters. The division is a tried and tested level of combat and removing it would place tremendous stress at the Corps level.

This organisational change notwithstanding, the PLA today has 18 Group Armies. Of these, the 38 and 39 group armies of the Shenyang and Beijing MACs are Rapid Reaction Forces. Another three group armies, one each in the Shenyang, Lanzhou and Jinan MAC are being modernised for modern mobile warfare missions. Four to five group armies in the Nanjing and Guangzhou MAC are focused on amphibious warfare. In sum, these forces, along with the 15 Air Borne Corps and two marine divisions, represent the ground combat force of the PLA.[28]

The outline order of battle (ORBAT) of PLA is as under:

- Beijing MAC-27, Central Theatre Command—27, 38 and 65 Group Armies(GA);
- Chengdu MAC, Western Theatre Command—13 and 14 GAs;
- Guangzhou MAC, Southern Theatre Command—41 and 42 GAs;
- Jinan MAC, Northern Theatre Command—20, 26, and 54 GAs;
- Lanzhou MAC, Western Theatre Command—21 and 47 GAs;
- Nanjing MAC, Eastern Theatre Command—1, 12 and 31 GAs;
- Shenyang MAC—Central Theatre Command—16, 39 and 40 GAs.

Order of Battle (ORBAT)

PLA land forces consist of approximately 1.25-1.50 million soldiers spread over 7 Military Regions (five theatre Commands) in 18 Group Armies, approximately 18 Motorised Infantry Divisions, 8 Mechanised Infantry Divisions, 9 Armoured Divisions, 22 Motorised Infantry Brigades, 6 Mechanised Infantry Brigades and 9 Armoured Brigades. Apart from these, the PLA has a large number of reservists who would continue definitely in the rolls beyond 2030. The details of formations under each MAC are elucidated for correct comprehension of the force level. Though joint theatre commands are being formed it is important to understand these organisations to connect issues correctly.

Shenyang MAC, Northern Theatre Command

- 16th Group Army (Changchun, Jilin): This comprises two motorised divisions and two motorised brigades.
- 39th Group Army (Liaoyang, Liaoning). This is a Rapid Reaction Force. Its force level consists of two mechanised infantry divisions, an armoured division and one helicopter regiment.
- 40th Group Army (Jinzhou, Liaoning). This Group Army has no divisions. It has a force structure of three brigades, two motorised and one armoured brigade.

Beijing MAC, Central Theatre Command

- 27th Group Army (Shijiazhuang, Hubei): As the 40th Group Army, this is brigade based. It comprises two motorised brigades, two mechanised infantry brigades and one armoured brigade.
- 38th Group Army (Baoing, Hebei). Rapid Reaction Force which has a mix of divisions and brigades. It comprises two mechanised infantry divisions, one armoured brigade and one helicopter regiment.
- 65th Group Army (Zhangjiakou, Hebei): This comprises of one infantry division, one armoured division and one motorised infantry brigade.

Lanzhou MAC, Western Theatre Command

- 21st Group Army (Baoji, Shaanxi). This consists of one infantry division and one armoured division.
- 47th Group Army (Lintopng, Shaanxi). This is again based purely on brigades. Comprises of two motorised infantry brigades, one mechanised infantry brigade and one armoured brigade.
- Xinjiang Military District. This has approximately four additional divisions, 12 Border Defence Regiments and two PAP division.

Jinan MAC (currently combined with Chengdu Military Region, Western Theatre Command)

- 20th Group Army (Kaifeng, Henan). This is a mechanised Group Army with one motorised brigade, one mechanised infantry brigade and one armoured brigade.

- 26th Group Army (Weifang, Shandong). A mixed composition comprising three motorised infantry brigades, one armoured division and one helicopter regiment.
- 54th Group Army (Xinjiang, Henan). A mechanised formation with one motorised division, one mechanised infantry division, one armoured division and one helicopter regiment.

Nanjing MAC, Eastern Theatre Command

- 1st Group Army (Huzhou, Zhejiang). A Group Army with amphibious capabilities comprising one amphibious division, one motorised infantry division, one armoured division and one helicopter regiment.
- 12th Group Army (Xuzhou, Jiangsu). This consists of three motorised infantry brigades and one armoured division.
- 31st Group Army ((Xiamen, Fujian). This formation again has the amphibious capability. It comprises two motorised infantry divisions, one motorised infantry brigade, one amphibious armoured brigade and one helicopter regiment.

Guangzhou MAC, Southern Theatre Command

- 41st Group Army (Liuzhou, Guangxi). This comprises of one infantry division, one motorised infantry division and one armoured brigade.
- 42nd Group Army (Huizhou, Guangdong). This Group Army has the amphibious capability. It comprises of one amphibious mechanised infantry division, one infantry division, one armoured brigade and one helicopter regiment.

Chengdu MAC (now Combined with Lanzhou MAC), Western Theatre Command

- 13th Group Army (Chongqing). This comprises two infantry divisions, one armoured brigade and one helicopter regiment.
- 14th Group Army (Kunming, Yunnan). This comprises two infantry divisions and one armoured brigade.
- Tibet Military District. This consists of a mixed force of two motorised infantry brigades, one mechanised infantry brigade, two PAP Divisions, and four Border Defence Regiments.[29]

Resolving Emergency Mobile Combat Forces (REMCF) (Kuiaisa Fanyin Budui) or RRFs

The PLA began raising its Rapid reaction forces (RRFs) in the late 1980s. A 100,000 strong fully mechanised REMCF was established in 1992 and placed under the direct control of the CMC. It was tasked for Border defence, dealing with internal armed conflict; maintenance of public order and conducting disaster relief operations. To create this REMCF, each PLA Group Army of every MR selected an Infantry Division to be designated as REMCF for dealing with emergency situations in any of the MRs.

The second tri-service REMCF which was to be 300,000 strong was raised in 1998 and also placed under direct command of the CMC. This consisted of:

- 15th Air Borne Corps ex-PLAAF;
- 5th Amphibious Landing Division—PLAN;
- 91 and 121 Divisions ex PLA;
- 15 AB Corps: The 15th AB Corps has the 43, 44 and 45 Air Borne Divisions deployed as follows:
    - 43 AB Div: Stationed at Kaifeng in Hunan province, it is attached to Jinan MR.
    - 44 AB Div: Stationed at Yin-shin in Hubei province, it is attached to Lanzhou MR and as such could be employed in Ladakh.
    - 45 AB Div: Stationed in Huangpi in Hubei province, is also attached to the Lanzhou MR—and could also see employment in Ladakh.

Though this is a strategic reserve force, it could yet be deployed in tactical terms as a light advance force—an Airmobile RRF or virtually a reconnaissance strike complex that initiates operations. Other important RRFs are:

- 38 Group Army (Beijing MR) has the 112, 113 and 114 Divs (one armoured and 3 mechanised divisions) designated as REMCF.
- 39 Group Army (Shenyang MR) has the 115, 116 and 190 Divisions (1 x armoured and 3 x mechanised divisions) designated as REMCF.
- 127 Mech Inf Div (ex 54 Group Army, Jinan MR).
- 149 Mech Inf Div (ex 13 Group Army, Chengdu MR).
- 7 x Special Operational Force Groups—one in each MR.
- PLAN First Marine Brigade (South China Sea Fleet).

The PLA has one regimental level army special force brigade deployed in each MR and serves as an RRF unit directly under a MR HQ Commander. The commander, political commissar and chief of staff of this special forces regiment are all full colonels. All officers above platoon commanders are university level graduates who receive further military education at the Army Command Academy.

Deployment against India

It is essential to estimate the forces that could be deployed against India in an adverse situation. Historically, the Chinese 2nd Field Army under Marshal Liu Bo Cheng had annexed Tibet in 1950. The 18th Corps of the 2nd Field Army was deployed for this task. 133 Infantry Division ex 46 Corps was also placed under its command. During the Sino-Indian conflict in 1962, the Chinese used acclimatised troops. The forces deployed against India were the three divisions of 18 Corps and 133 Infantry Div ex 46 Corps. Later the balance two divisions ex 46 Corps was also pushed in for phase two of the offensive. A division minus under Major General He Jiachen was employed ex Xinjiang MR in Ladakh.

Currently, the Tibet Military District comes under both the Lanzhou and Chengdu MAC, which would be part of the Western Theatre Command. In the present reorganisation, they form a part of the Western Theatre Command. During operations, it is likely that a War Zone Command will come up in Lhasa and function directly under the CMC in Beijing. It will have the authority to command troops and aircraft resources of both MACs of Lanzhou and Chengdu (Reorganised as Western Theatre Command). Thus India would face two MACs with their group armies plus the REMCF of the 15 Air Borne Corps. The group armies are capable of the independent frontal strike, deep penetration and fast encirclement from all directions. At least one group army in each MR has an aviation regiment. The designated RRFs for Tibet are:

- 49 Division of 13 Group Army ex Chengdu MR: of Western Theatre Command. This specialises in mountain warfare and is tasked to safeguard the Sino-Indian border.
- 62 Division of 21st Group Army ex Lanzhou MR of Western Theatre Command: This trains regularly for high altitude warfare.

All air elements of the PLAAF in the MRs would also come under command.

The three traditional airfields in Tibet have been Hoping, Pangta and Kongka Dzong. In addition, new airfields have been commissioned in Lhasa and Nagachuka and these could be activated rapidly. Five more airfields are being completed at Ngari Gunsa, Ati, Naqu, Lokha and Shigatse. These will help to rapidly induct RRFs. However, the PLAAF could at best support one and a half Air Divisions (4 to 5 Air regiments in Tibet). The PLAAF's medium-range aviation based in Kunming could interdict the Brahmaputra Valley and the Aviation in Xinjiang could interdict the Indus Valley.

India-centric Chengdu and Lanzhou MRs (Being reorganised as Western Theatre Command)

Lanzhou MAC is a far stronger and has better equipped group armies than the Chengdu MAC. It has access to far greater levels of integral airpower. It would be natural to expect the greater weight of attack in the Ladakh Sector than perhaps in Arunachal Pradesh. It is noteworthy that Ladakh is the only province where China and Pakistan can conduct coordinated operations. The PLA and PLAAF have held a number of joint army-air exercises opposite Ladakh and Uttarakhand in the last two years. Brigade-level live-fire exercises involving tank attacks on passes at 5,000 metres have been conducted in concert with close air support and large scale employment of artillery with smart munitions, MBRLs and conventional tipped missiles (Non-Line of Sight, Battlefield support Missiles—NLOS—BSMs). These include the 300 mm PH1-65 MBRLs and Type 90—122mm MBRLs. PLZ-67 122mm tracked SP Howitzers have also been employed in exercises along with Type 96G MBTs with 125mm smooth bore guns and 1,000 HP engines. The Type 86G ICV with a 30mm automatic cannon and NORINCO HJ-73 wire-guided ATGM of the three-kilometer range have also been employed.[30]

The PLA is experimenting with joint operations. It is likely that one division in the Lanzhou MR and both the brigades of Chengdu MR Division and along with the 33 Air Division of the PLAAF in Chengdu MR have been assigned the duties of experimentation in integrated Joint operations.[31] The 139 Mechanised Division in Xinjiang is also testing new equipment like heli-portable all-terrain vehicles and working closely with helicopter units in air mobile operations training. The PLA recently constructed two of the world's biggest heli-bases in the Aksai-Chin area, opposite Ladakh. These can accommodate up to 300 medium-lift helicopters as also attack helicopters that will be based at 22,000 feet altitude. These heli-bases are designed to facilitate the deployment of the REMCFs. It has also established a massive ELINT/Signal Intelligence station in Aksai Chin to conduct Electronic Warfare and border surveillance missions. These REMCFs could threaten Indian Army positions in Sub Sector North (SSN), Sub Sector West (SSW) and the Saltoro Ridge in the Siachen Glacier.[32]

So far China had not acquired helicopters in large numbers as envisaged by its RRF/REMCF concept. Even its Air Borne Corps could at best lift up to one Air Borne Division and heli-lift a brigade at a time. All this is likely to change rapidly. China has just recently signed a deal to build under license some 1,000 medium-lift helicopters. Cooperation for joint development for a medium-sized, highly capable, the twin-engine helicopter was started in 2005 between Avicopter of China and Airbus Helicopters of France. In 2014, a deal for joint production of 1000 twin-engine A-352 / EC-175 helicopters was signed during President Xi Jinping's visit to France. Avicopter will produce these helicopters for China under the designation AC 352. Air Bus will produce them in France as the EC-175 for the world market and initial deliveries are expected to commence in the current year. This helicopter is designed to meet a whole range of missions, including offshore crew transport, search and rescue, casualty evacuation and utility roles. Details of the exact numbers of helicopters China will produce are yet to emerge clearly but helicopters will soon be available to the PLA ground forces in much larger numbers than heretofore and will help to actualise the basal concept of the RRFs and facilitate SOF operations. The helipads for large scale employment of helicopters have already been constructed opposite Ladakh.[33]

The highly mountainous and rugged terrain of Xinjiang and Tibet is not really suitable for the deployment of heavy mechanised forces. As such, China has gone in for light mechanised forces based on NORINCO built WMZ-550 (four-wheeled), WMZ-551 (6 wheeled) and WMZ-525 (8 wheeled) armoured personnel carriers along with WMZ-551A (Type 92) and WMZ-561 (Type 86) by PLZ-95 Class AD gun/missile carrier tracked vehicles; ZW-10A attack helicopters and WS-13 MBRLs.

The 6th Highland Mechanized Division is the REMCF (RRF) of the Lanzhou MAC and will most likely be one of the first formations to be employed in Ladakh. It has three mechanised infantry brigades, an armoured brigade, an artillery brigade, an AD brigade, a helicopter wing and a logistics brigade. The equipment profile of this formation is as under:

- Armour—99 x Type 96 MBTs;
- AIFVs—351 x Type 86 AIFVs;
- Artillery—72 x 155mm cal SP Gun PLZ-05;
- Air Defense (AD):
    - AD Platoon of 3 x PLZ-95s with SHORAD Missiles
    - 27 x Motorised AD vehicles with 108 x SHORAD missile launcher
- The AD Brigade has:
    - 1 Battalion Towed 57mm AD Gun;
    - 1 Battalion Towed 30mm AD Gun;
    - 1 Platoon of PLZ-95s.
- Helicopter Wing—6 x Harbin 2-9G Attack helicopters; and 6 x M-17US helicopters.

Each group army has a battalion level special reconnaissance task force unit. Officers and men of these units are handpicked and the wastage rate is almost 50 per cent. These special units are rehearsed in:

- Occupying and defending key points;
- Sabotaging airfields;
- Anti-air Attack;
- Anti-Reconnaissance and Surveillance Tasks.

The RRF units are currently deployed in the Tibetan Autonomous Region (TAR) and specialise in the conduct of recce combat operations. These involve the use of signal intelligence, helicopters (air-mobile, armed aero scout and attack) along with high mobility reconnaissance teams that will provide actionable intelligence for light mechanised infantry formations. These serve as blocking forces to ambush and halt retreating enemy ground elements. They not only act as ground-based interdiction forces but also provide fire coordination for long-range field artillery and tactical air support. Thus in the entire Tibetan theatre, we are likely to see extensive employment of special task forces carrying out the role of reconnaissance-strike complexes and focus light mechanised forces on to the objectives they will engage, bypass and interdict. Encirclement and annihilation of enemy formations still remain the prime focus of Chinese ground operations.

Army aviation units were raised in April 1986. These were used for reconnaissance, anti-armour operations, insertion of Special Forces, electronic counter measures and relocation of command elements. The Chinese have custom built the ZA-10A twin-engine Light Attack Helicopter (this has Canadian engines). Currently, the primary workhorse is the Russian designed Mi-17V helicopter. These have the severe limitation of greatly curtailed payloads beyond 10,000 feet. The Chinese had some 250 helicopters of all types in 1990 (Mi-4, Mi-8 & some Mi-17s). By 2011, China had enhanced its helicopter fleet to 500 out of which some 200 are modern machines like Mi-17 and indigenous Z-9. The Chinese Army Aviation is now poised for a major takeoff. The Chinese have in 2014 concluded an agreement for the license manufacture of some 1,000 helicopters. These will give a tremendous fillip to the Chinese reconnaissance-strike complexes and help in very speedy induction of Rapid Reaction Forces. With the induction of a sizeable number of helicopters, army aviation will play an increasingly important role in Chinese ground operations. From being a support force it aims at becoming a "main battle assault force". These forces to operate would need a favourable air situation. It is important that the PLAAF provides a favourable air situation to enable helicopters to operate smoothly.

A number of Chinese web sites and official media sources indicate that Chinese local forces comprise of some:

- 57 Border Defence Regiments and 9 Border Defence Battalions;
- Four Patrol Craft Groups for riverine operations;
- Two Coastal Defence Divisions, three Coastal defence brigades.

Thus overall some 200,000 personnel are assigned to permanent border guarding and coastal defence responsibility. These have infantry and artillery units as also Silkworm cruise missiles.

The overall army reserve units number approximately 40 divisions, 25 brigades and several regiments. A new development is the creation of a logistic reserve brigade in each MR. Now, reserve AA brigades and AA regiments have been reported in the Chinese media. One-third of the PLA reserve divisions and brigades are AA units, indicating the primacy of the air defence tasking in the depth areas as also the task of repair of rail and road infrastructure by these reserve units and formations in response to enemy air attacks designed to interdict the Chinese communications in wartime.

It is pertinent to note that the Chinese fought their last war in 1979 against Vietnam. This was a relatively limited conflict and lasted barely a month. Today, therefore, virtually no member of the armed forces possesses any war fighting experience. This has the potential to become a significant disadvantage in an armed conflict against experienced armed forces. Military modernisation in the Chinese armed forces is proceeding asymmetrically. While some units may use cutting edge technology that provides war fighting superiority it is almost certain that large parts of the armed forces keep outdated and inoperable equipment and have a low standard of training. Therefore despite their superiority in technology and numbers, they lack combat experience which would be a significant factor in gauging their relative strength.[34] By 2030 the PLA would be a versatile military adversary for India to contend. There is an obvious need for India to match Chinese military capabilities.

Logistical Aspects

Golmud-Lhasa Rail Line: This 1,118-kilometre-long railway line (Qinghai Tibet Railway—QTR) has tripled China's logistical capability and offensive power in Tibet. The REMCF from Gansu and Shanxi provinces can now be deployed by rail in less than twelve hours for limited offensive tasks against Indian forces in Sikkim and Arunachal Pradesh (ALP). Reinforcements from Beijing and Shenyang MRs can now reach the Tibet Autonomous Region within 20 hours instead of the earlier 80 hours. This railway line has 32 railway stations en route and can take eight trains per day. Each train can bring in a battalion group. This route has over 30 tunnels and bridges that cover a distance of 37.5 km. This is a standard gauge rail line and can carry tanks, howitzers and missiles. Each train has two up rated diesel-electric engines and pressurised cabins for operation in High Altitude Areas (HAA). On August 15, 2014 China extended the railway line by 253-kilometres from Lhasa to Shigatse close to the Indian border at Sikkim. It takes two hours to cover this distance which is indeed faster than the fastest train in India. China has also unveiled plans to construct a railway line from Lhasa to Nyingchi which is close to Arunachal Pradesh.[35]

The simple fact is that in the 1980s, the low-level Chinese threat from Tibet was reckoned as six divisions and the high-level as 22 divisions. However, given the state of the infrastructure in Tibet then, this force level could only be built up over two seasons. Hence a major build-up would have taken two years and given more than adequate warning. With the Golmud-Lhasa rail line, the Chinese can now build up over 30 divisions in just about a month's time. This rail line can carry five million tons of goods each year. The entire Chinese threat via Tibet has undergone a paradigm shift enabling China to rapidly mobilise in Tibet. China is now constructing three additional rail lines into Tibet. These are as stated:

- Lanzhou-Nagchu—Lhasa;
- Chengdu- Kongpo—Lhasa;
- Dali- Nyingtri—Lhasa.

These new rail lines are likely to be completed by 2038.

The Chinese have three major road highways coming into Tibet. These will be substantially modernised by 2020:

- Central Highway (1,154 km): The Gormo-Lhasa cl-50 road can transport some 3,520 tons of loads each day.
- Eastern Highway (3,105 km): The Chengdu-Lhasa road cl-18 can transport 800 tons a day.
- Western Highway: This is a cl-18 to cl-50 road that runs 150 km in depth from the Indian border. It can carry 800 tons of loads per day.

In 2003, the Chinese had started a major road up-gradation program that resulted in the up gradation of 51,000 km of roads in Tibet by the time of the Beijing Olympics in 2008. By 2008, all roads in this region were two-way blacktop roads. The Central Highway to Lhasa is now four lane and all main arteries are all-weather and designed to remain open throughout the year. Another 7,000 km of highways in Tibet were upgraded by 2010. The current target is to increase the existing network of highways from the current 58,000 km to 70,000 km by 2015. With this, the Chinese road network would have the capacity to carry some 11,000 tons per day. By 2030, all roads would be all weather and enable movement possibly all around the year.[36]

Oil pipeline. The Gormo-Lhasa oil pipeline is 1,080 km in length and can supply 500,000 tons of oil annually.[37]

Airfields. There is a total of eight airfields in Tibet. Of these five are currently operational, two are under construction and one is in a state of disuse. Active air bases are Shiquanhe, Shigatse, Tsethang, Nyingchi and Naqu. Besides this, there are six major airfields in Xinjiang. These include: Hotan, Kashgar, Korla, Urumqi and Yarkand. These air-bases are currently being used by civil aviation and do not have blast pens and limited apron facilities. However, PLAAF aircraft regularly carry out training sorties from these bases. In all, there are some 18 airfields in the Tibet–Xinjiang region from where SU-27 aircraft could strike India. Reports indicate that an additional 22 airfields are to be constructed in this region by 2020. The daily tonnages available in Tibet would work out as under:

- Rail—9,300 tons per day.
- Road—11,500 tons per day.
- Air—1000 tons per day.

The main logistics feed stations are in Chengdu and Lanzhou MACs (Western Theatre Command). The Chinese solution is in the form of five to six logistics brigades in the Tibet (Xijang) Military District. These can hold fuel and commodities stocks. Each logistics brigade supports an infantry heavy group army. Thus logistically, the Chinese can easily sustain 18 divisions plus in Tibet. This helps to overcome the logistical weakness of the Chinese Divisions that have a very low stock/store holding capacity. Chinese divisions run out of ammunition/essential supplies in seven to ten days of combat and are forced to go for standard logistical pauses that are fairly predictable. These Chinese logistics brigades try and overcome this problem. In contrast, the Indian Mountain Divisions have major maintenance areas and can hold impressive amounts of stocks.

Points Meriting Attention

The First Gulf War was a major shock for the PLA and showed how unprepared it was to deal with the new RMA. Chinese defence expenditure went up seven-fold from US$ 17.9 billion to a whopping US$ 129.3 billion between 1990 and 2011. It was US$ 150 billion in 2017. The emphasis has been on downsizing and modernisation.

PLA forces have been restructured, beginning with the conversion of infantry divisions into infantry-heavy combined arms brigade in the late 1990s.

Table 3.1: Changes in Force Level[39]
Changes in the Chinese Army Manoeuvre Units since 1997

Ser No.	Formations	1997	2011
1.	Group Armies	24	18
2.	Infantry Division	90	26
3.	Armoured Divisions	12	7-9
4.	Infantry Brigades	7	28-31
5.	Armoured Brigades	13	9-11
6.	Helicopter Regiments/Brigades	7/0	9/4
7.	Special Operations Groups/Regiments	7/0	8/1

The new brigades include three to four infantry battalions, a battalion of tanks, a battalion of artillery and other combat support capabilities. The restructuring implies cost saving and revised command and control relationships, besides revised training regimes. Doing away with the divisional-level command and control is a far-reaching decision and may well come back to haunt the PLA in its next major engagements. Copying the US Army that is tailored for expeditionary warfare may not suit continental warfare needs in Asia.

Overall Military Equipment Profile PLA

The entire emphasis now is on overall force reduction and downsizing with the modernisation of forces on the basis of Islands of Excellence in terms of RRFs. The emphasis is on trans-regional mobility mostly via the high-speed rail network to mass forces. From 1990 onwards, the PLA has begun to move drastically away from its motivated manpower emphasis paradigm, to a western way of warfighting heavily premised upon technological superiority and combined—arms—warfare. All this is so very far removed from the PLAs traditional roots and it remains to be seen how the PLA will fare in this high-tech, all-arms coordinated way of war.

The drastic downsizing of the PLA that would ensue from a full conversion of its formations from the classical Corps based on three divisions to a corps composed of brigades with no intermediate divisional headquarters on the lines of United States forces. It seems premised upon a wholly offensive orientation of the PLA which stems from the baseline presumption that its hold upon the initiative will be complete and total in all circumstances and against all occasions. The American contagion had initially infected the Indian

Table 3.2: Equipment Profile[40]

Ser No.	Equipment type	1990	2011	Modern Type	Recent models
1.	Transport helicopters	250	500	(200)	Russian Mi-17 and Chinese Z-9
2.	Attack helicopters	60	110	(10)	Z-10 China AH
3.	Tanks	7,750	7,050	(2,000)	Type 96 and Type 98/99
4.	Infantry Fighting Vehicles (IFV) and Armoured Personnel Carriers (APCs)	2,800	5,090	(2,250)	Type 97 IFVWZ-551 series
5.	Artillery	18,300	8,000	(1,710)	120mm mortar122, 152 and 155mm SP Howitzers

Army because copying the Americans has always been fashionable. The Indian Army, however, overcame its downsizing, imitative impulse due to its extensive commitment in counterinsurgency operations. Currently, the Indian Army is also undertaking four studies to right size the army. Strangely, the PLA has not overcome this imitative fixation even after the Americans themselves have painfully re-learnt the value of boots on the ground after Gulf War-II. At long last, the Indian Army has come out of its defensive-minded rut in the Himalayas. This is exemplified by the raising of two additional defensive divisions in the North-East and now a new strike corps for the mountains. If India is able to complete its long-pending infrastructure creation in the Himalayas and not waste inordinate amounts of time in raising the mountain strike corps, it could seriously dislocate the Chinese design of battle in the mountains.

It is pertinent to note that China is following the US example of employing armour in the Himalayas. Light armour could be used with intelligence and dexterity in the mountainous regions as demonstrated by the PLA in current exercises. The moot point is for India to suitably equip its formations to deal with this issue. Chinese logistics by 2030 will enable them to fight a full-fledged battle with its entire inventory of state of the art equipment.

Xi Jinping and PLA Reforms

The year 2016 witnessed President Xi Jinping unleashing military reforms to enhance modernisation and improve Jointness between the forces. The changes would enable China to fight a network centric war with synergy between organisations. These stem from the Chinese White Paper of 2015. The major changes are stated below:

- The CMC would directly take charge of the administration of the PLA and integrated battle zone commands would be created to focus on combat. The CMC would have a Joint Staff Department, Political Works Department, Logistics Support Department, Training and Administration Department, Mobilisation Department, Discipline Inspection Commission, Political and Law Commission, Science and Technology Commission, Office of Strategic Planning, Reform and Organisational Structure Department, International Military Cooperation, Audit Office and an Agency for Office Administration.
- The PLA has been restructured and would comprise of the PLA Army (PLAA), PLA Navy (PLAN), PLA Air Force (PLAAF), the erstwhile Second Artillery has become PLA Rocket Force (PLARF) and the PLA Strategic Support Force (PLASSF) which would undertake Cyber, Space and Electronic Warfare.
- The seven Military Regions have been replaced by five Theatre Commands Northern, Western, Southern, Eastern and Central Command. Tibet will come under the Western Command and the Headquarters will be at Lanzhou. These are being formed to undertake joint operations.
- In addition, there would be a reduction of manpower by 300,000 personnel by 2017.

Overall there would be no reduction in the Group Armies and each Command would be able to undertake joint operations. A map showing the Geographical Area of responsibility is given. It would be observed that the Indian Borders would be tackled by the Western Theatre Command.[41]

The map gives the geographical areas for the newly formed joint commands who would be formed in the near future. Broadly, the Western Command will be responsible for India, the Southern Command for Vietnam, The Eastern Command for Taiwan, the Central Command for Japan and Northern Command for Russia.

CHINA'S NEW THEATER COMMANDS

Figure 3.6: Map Showing New Joint Commands[42]

Impact of PLA Reforms on the Indian Armed Forces

PLA Reforms: Initial Phase—31 December 2015 and January 2016

The current reforms are related directly to the Chinese Defence White Paper on Strategy in Perspective which was published in 2015. The main theme for this White Paper has been its focus on Jointness, particularly in view of the Rebalancing Policy of the United States in the Asia Pacific Region. In order to address these current challenges, the White Paper explicitly states that "The traditional mentality that land outweighs sea, must be abandoned and great importance has to be attached to managing the seas and oceans and protecting maritime rights and interests."

It implies that the PLA Navy would be involved with open seas protection in conjunction with the PLA Air Force. The development possibly is linked to the announcement in November 2013 at the Third Plenary session of the 18th Chinese Communist Party Central Committee that CMC must exercise

Joint Command Authority over the three services and the system of Joint Theatre Command will be introduced. The issues were further reiterated by Xi Jinping on 31 December 2015, when he ceremonially inaugurated the three new Services of the PLA with their military flags. Broadly, the reforms are to improve theoretical and technological innovation, restructuring of the organisation to fight in an age of information.

The first aspect is to clarify is that the three new services are the PLA Land Army (PLAA), the PLA Rocket Forces (PLARF) and the PLA Strategic Support Forces (PLASSF). The land forces would be the army component of the PLA, the PLARF would be the erstwhile Second Artillery of China and the PLASSF would be undertaking aspects pertaining to Cyber Warfare and Outer Space. The PLA Land Army would have a separate headquarters like the Navy and the Air Force. The PLARF is a rechristened version of the erstwhile Second Artillery of the PLA. The force is upgraded to the same status as the Navy and Air Force. The overall structure remains the same. The PLASSF is a high technology force with its focus on information warfare. This organisation would focus on space operations to include reconnaissance and navigational satellites. Further, it would combat Electronic Warfare and Cyber Warfare. The PLASSF puts the PLA in the era of hi-tech combat forces.

Closely following the formation of the three new services was the restructuring of the CMC in mid-January 2016. The erstwhile four departments of the CMC have been reconfigured into six functional departments, three commissions and six offices. The six departments are Joint Staff, Political Work, Logistical Support, Equipment Development, Training & Administration Department and National Defence Mobilisation Department. The three Commissions are Discipline Inspection, Politics & Law and Science and Technology Commission. The six offices are the General Office, Administration, Auditing, International Cooperation, Reform & Organisation Structure and Strategic Planning Offices. The orders were given on 10 January 2016. These departments replace the General Staff, General Political, General Logistics and General Armament Departments.

The CMC would provide the leadership and command over the entire PLA. The entire control of all elements would come under the Chairman of the CMC. In the CMC, the Joint Staff Department would be tasked to carry out operational planning, operational logistics and formulate a strategy for undertaking military operations. The Political Work Department would be responsible for the political orientation of the entire armed forces. It is pertinent to note that the PLA belongs and comes under the Communist Party of China and there is a political commissar in each formation, unit, warship, air base, missile base and training establishments. The Logistics Support Department would be responsible for the overall logistics of the PLA and the Equipment Development Department would deal with Research & Development as also acquisition and maintenance of military equipment. The Training and Administration Department would look after the leadership training of the PLA and the training establishments. The National Defence Mobilisation Department would boost the quality of the reserve system to enable speedy mobilisation of reserves.

The three Commissions in the CMC have a significant role to play in the governance of the PLA. First of all the Discipline and Inspection Commission will send inspection teams to various Theatre Commands of the PLA to keep a check on organisational cohesiveness. The Politics & Law Commission would work towards the enhancement of military governance and military law. Both these aspects are extremely important in a military set up. The Science and Technology Commission would be applying itself in the fields of defence technology. This commission would integrate developments in the civilian sector and have its accent on self-reliance and innovation.

The affiliated offices are to undertake the office aspects pertaining to the functions of the CMC. The Strategic Planning Office is to improve the strategic planning system. The reform and organisational structure office would be tasked to undertake military reforms. Military engagement and coordination would be undertaken by the International Military cooperation office. The other offices comprising audit and administration would undertake military audit and administration of the organisation of the CMC.

Next Phase Reforms—February 2016

China has been practising a War Zone style of undertaking operations since 2008. This primarily means optimising forces available to effect operations in a coherent manner. Often it has meant troops of more than one military region undertaking operations together. Keeping this in mind, China decided to form five theatre commands. On February 1, 2016, President Xi Jinping officially inaugurated the five theatre commands representing geographic directions. North, South, East. West and Central. The Northern Command headquarters is located at Shenyang, the Eastern Command at Nanjing, the Southern Command at Guangzhou, the Western Command at Chengdu and the Central Command at Beijing. Each theatre command is ready for Active Defence in comparison to the Military Regions being ready for multi-layered defence. The exact boundaries are yet to be promulgated and the assets regarding the PLAN and PLAAF have yet to be decided. All commanders belong to the Army. As per the Hong Kong Press, the North Sea Fleet is to be given to Central Theatre Command, the East Sea Fleet is likely to be allotted to Eastern Theatre Command and the South Sea Fleet is likely to be allotted to Southern Theatre Command. Though the exact boundaries are under consideration, a map showing the Theatre Commands is given in Fig 3.6 above.

As shown in the map, the Northern Command would be dealing with Mongolia, Russia and North Korea. The Central Command would be interested in both the Koreas. Japan and possibly be a reserve for operations being conducted in other regions. The Eastern Command would be focused on Taiwan. The Southern Command on Vietnam, Laos and Myanmar. The Western Command has a large continental border and would deal with India, Bhutan, Nepal, Pakistan, Afghanistan, Kazakhstan, Kyrgyzstan, Tajikistan and Southern Mongolia. If the maritime threat to India is concerned, it would be with the South Sea Fleet likely to be placed under Southern Command which would pose a threat to the Indian Ocean with further modernisation of the Chinese Navy.

Other Reforms

On September 3, 2015, Chinese President Xi Jinping announced that the PLA will reduce 300,000 troops. President Xi made the announcement just before attending a massive military parade in Beijing to commemorate the 70th anniversary of the end of World War II. This forms a part of the modernisation process where modern organisations call for an optimised rank and file. It is pertinent to note that even after the cutting of troops; China remains the largest armed forces in the world. The cuts will be made in a manner so as to cause minimum turbulence. The recruitment process would enlist lesser personnel and those compelled to leave would undergo skill development training to be absorbed in state-owned enterprises. Further, the

PLA continues to run a few business organisations despite Zhang Jemin's directions of 1998. Overall, the reforms are a continuation of the revolution in military affairs set up by the PLA after the First Gulf War.

Impact

A publication of the official China mouthpiece in November 2011, recommended that China adopt new approaches in dealing with its neighbours. It further stated that goodwill may not bring harmony and sometimes certain altercations with neighbours are appropriate and can result in the return of peace. China currently has clearly stated that its territorial claims are not negotiable and, in view of this, Indian Armed Forces have to be prepared for the worst scenario, which is a two-front war.

The current Chinese reforms have led to jointness and enabled it to undertake future operations in cyber warfare and outer space. There is a dire need for the Indian Armed Forces to integrate to stand up to the new reforms in the PLA. As per these reforms, the Western Command of China would face the Indian Army on its Northern and North Eastern borders. Threats from China have to be viewed also from the maritime angle and in this case, the Chinese Southern Command with the South Sea Fleet would be of importance to our country. From our side, we have to have a new force structure within a decade to match China's continental and maritime capabilities. We must understand that in the CMC there is a Chief of General Staff to coordinate all operations.

Currently, we don't have a joint structure to fight a two-front war. After the Kargil War, the K Subramanian Committee submitted its report for review by a Group of Ministers in 2000. To improve Jointness, a need was felt for a Chief of Defence Staff (CDS) and for integration of the three services. In the 17 years that have elapsed, we have established a tri-service headquarters of Integrated Defence Staff (IDS), a tri-service Andaman and Nicobar theatre command and a Strategic Forces Command. There is no jointness of command and control and the three services are operationally independent with limited coordination being undertaken by the Ministry of Defence. To find an answer to the current impasse, the government had appointed a 14-member task force on July 14, 2011 that was headed by former bureaucrat late Shri Naresh Chandra to review the unfinished tasks of the Kargil Review Committee and suggest a plan of implementation. It is learnt that the committee has recommended a permanent Chairman Chiefs of Staff Committee (PCCOSC) and joint theatre commands. There are reports in the print media which state that the government is possibly going ahead with the proposal of a PCCOSC who would be a four-star general. This would be the first step, but currently, there is no forward movement.

While this is being processed, being a democratic country, we must look at the American and the UK experience of integrating their armed forces. The first step is a Defence Policy Guideline. The US Secretary of Defense issues a Defence Policy Guideline which includes national security objectives and policies, the priorities of military missions and the availability of resources. This document is prepared with advice from the Chairman, Joint Chiefs of Staff. In our case, there is no National Strategic Policy. At best, a generic chapter on the national security environment is included. Today there is no single point military guidance on strategic matters to the defence minister and the prime minister. On most occasions, it is the defence secretary who coordinates military issues. This is certainly incorrect for a country fighting insurgency and dealing with sensitive borders. Presently there is no unified action and a lot depends on the individual perception of a situation which often leads to a lack of optimisation of resources in dealing with critical situations.

In our present context, a war against China would primarily involve the eastern portion of the country, where we have the Eastern Command of the army, navy and air force are located at Kolkata, Vishakapatnam and Shillong respectively. In the current environment, despite a PCCOSC, each service therefore would be fighting its own war. This is inappropriate and there is a need form a joint theatre command to counter China's Western Command.

Deductions

- The Gulf War was a wakeup call to the PLA. Deng, the visionary, commenced the modernisation process of the armed forces and to achieve global missile capability by 2030. The Chinese would be able to launch effective operations in all five dimensions and on sea, air, cyber and outer space
- China's armed forces in future would be equipped with state-of-the-

art weaponry to include Assassins Mace weapons. These would assist China in fighting a full-scale conventional conflict an asymmetric war under a nuclear overhang. The new military reforms initiated in February 2016 will help them enhance their Jointness in fighting battles on land, sea, air and in outer space

- The Chinese armed forces have modernised their doctrines and their organisations to launch effective operations if the need arises through the Lanzhou and Chengdu Military Regions. Further, ballistic and cruise missiles have been suitably deployed to engage targets in India
- China could also launch cyber-attacks, anti-satellite weapons, missiles and a ground offensive or multiple intrusions. Further, they could build up Pakistan and extend support to insurgents in North East India to keep the pot boiling.
- Intentions of China would be dictated by circumstances and the Indian armed forces have to be prepared to meet all eventualities
- New military reforms introduced in February 2016 will improve the jointness in the Chinese armed forces

Assessment

The Chinese armed forces are being modernised rapidly. However, the quality of their equipment and capabilities are certainly lower than claimed. United States officers posted in Pakistan have commented that Pakistanis have often changed the components of Chinese equipment with items from the Gulf countries. Further reforms in the armed forces takes a long time to fructify, As one can observe, all theatre commanders are from the PLA Army. Jointness will take time to be effective on the ground, may be about ten years. It takes about 20 years for a navy to fine tune aircraft carrier and submarine operations. Their indigenisation process is based on copying and reverse engineering, and it would take some time before they learn to innovate.

The last war that China fought was in 1979. Their army performed poorly in the conflict against Vietnam. Their generalship has not been tested and their performance in the cyber and space domain needs qualitative improvement. By contrast, the Indian armed forces are skilled, experienced and combat hardened. Further, they are striving hard to modernise at a deliberate pace. Accuracy and consistency will determine the result of future conflicts. India is prepared to meet China in terms of capabilities.

NOTES

1. David Shambaugh, "Modernising China's Military Progress, Problems and Prospects", *University of California Press*, Berkley, 2002, pp.2-3.
2. Image of Deng Xiao Ping, money week.com, published on 22 July 1977.
3. Bates Gill, "China and the Revolution on Military Affairs: Assessing Economic and Socio-Cultural Factors", *Strategic Studies Institute, US Army War College* Occasional Papers, 20 May 1996, pp.2-33. Ibid, p.3.
4. Alistar Ian Johnson, "Prospects for Chinese Modernisation, Limited Deterrence versus Multilateral Arms Control", quoting Lin Zhaochang in the *China Quarterly*, No 146, June 1996, p.554.
5. Asian Military Review, Volume 8/Issue 8, December 2000/January 2001, p.42.
6. Anthony H Cordsman and Martin Kleiber, "Chinese Military Modernisation and Force Development", August 2006, p.40.
7. Ibid, p.760.
8. P K Chakravorty, "Firepower 2030", *KW Publishers*, New Delhi 2013, p.40.
9. Air Cmde Ramesh. Phadke, "Defending Indian Skies against the PLAAF", Indian Defence Review, January-March 2012,*Lancers Publishers and Distributors,* pp.39-45.
10. Robert.S. Norris and Hams. M. Kristensen, "Chinese Nuclear Forces 2006", http://the bulletin.metapress.com/content/1wo35m8u644p864u.
11. PLAAF, Military Balance, International Institute of Security Studies, London, 2011.
12. Richard D Fisher Jr, "China's Military Modernisation, Building for Regional and Global Reach", *Pentagon Press*, New Delhi, 2009, pp 81-89.
13. Images of Chinese Missile and Missile Inventory, Asia Eye Blog Project.2049/04/expansion of ballistic missile base.
14. Sean O'Connor, "Technical Report APA-TR—2009-1204", PLA Second Artillery Corps, www. ausairpowernet/APA-PLA-second Artillery-htmtl. 2009
15. Same as 13.
16. Same as 12.
17. William Atkins, "Chinese Beidou Navigation Satellite launched from Long March 3A", www.itwire.com/sciencenews/space/9201-chinese-Beidou-navigation-satellite launched from long march-3a-rocket.
18. Dhruv Katoch, "China's Defence Policy, Indian perspective, Implications for India", CLAWS, *KW Publishers*, New Delhi, 2011, pp. 146-147.
19. Ralph D. Sawyer, "The Seven Military Classics of Ancient China including Sun Tzu's Art of War", *West View Press Inc*, Boulder, Colorado USA, 1993.
20. Military Balance, International Institute of Strategic Studies, Routledge, London, 2014.
21. Edward Wong, Liu Huaqing, New York Times, New York, USA, www. nytimes.com, 16 January 2011.
22. Image of J-10 aircraft, www.militarytoday.com/aircraft/j10.
23. David Choi, "Image of J-20 aircraft", Business Insider, www.businessinsider.in, 25 July 2016.
24. David.M Finkelstein, "China's National Military Strategy", RAND Corporation,www.rand.org/content/dam/rand/pubs/conf.../CF145/CF145.chap7.pdf.
25. Paul.H.Godwin, "Chinese Military Strategy Revised; Local and Limited Wars", Annals of the American Academy of Political and Social Science, Volume 519, January 1994, pp. 191-201

and Changing Concepts of Doctrine, "Strategy and Operations of PLA, 1978-1987, China Quarterly No: 112, December 1987, pp. 578-581.

26. Harold Brown, Joseph W Prueher, Adam Segal, "Report of an Independent Task Force on Chinese Military Power," *Council of Foreign Relations*, 58 East, 68th Street, New York, www.cfr.org, 2003. pp. 38-51.

27. Central Committee of Communist Party of China, "The Chinese Dream infuses socialism with Chinese characteristics with new energy, Qiushi. China copy right and media. *Wsordpress.com*, 9 June 2013.

28. Anthony H Cordesman, "Chinese Military Modernisation and Force Development, Chinese and Outside Perspectives," Draft prepared for Arab Centre for Research and Policy Studies, conference for Arab, US Relations in Doha, June 2014, pp 153 to162.

29. Office of the Secretary of Defence, "Annual Report to Congress, Military and Security Developments involving the People's Republic of China," May 2012; http://www.defense.gov/pubs/pdfs/2012 CMPR Final.pdf and Dennis J Blasko, "The Chinese Army Today: Tradition and Transformation for the 21st Century,2nd edition, *Routledge*, New York, 2011, pp 87-102.

30. Cortez A Cooper, "RAND Report", 2006, Chapter-6, pp. 256-263 and "PLA Army Units in Chengdu Military Region, www.china-defense-mashup.com/china.../pla-army-units-in-chengdu-militia.

31. Kevin McCauley, "PLA Joint Operations Development and Military Reforms", China Brief, *The Jamestown Foundation*, Washington D.C. Volume 14, Issue 7, 2013.

32. Prasun K Gupta, "What China Really wants, "Opinion, Indiatvnews.com, 02 May 2013.

33. S. Chery, "Air Bus Helicopters and China's Aircopter sign joint production agreement for 1000 EC 175/A C 352 helicopter press release at airbushelicopters.com, 25 March 2014.

34. Anthony H Cordesman, "Chinese Military Modernisation and Force Development, Chinese and Outside Perspectives," Draft prepared for Arab Centre for Research and Policy Studies, conference for Arab, US Relations in Doha, June 2014, Chapter 8, pp. 198 to 222.

35. NDTV India, "China inaugurates new Tibet rail link close to Sikkim," NDTV, Convergence, New Delhi, www.ndtv.com, 15 August, 2014.

36. Press Trust of India, "China to build more Highways in Tibet," *The Times of India*, times of india.indiatimes.com, World, 26 July 2014.

37. Major General Sheru Thaplyal, "Infrastructural Developments in India-China Border Areas: A Comparison,"www.observerindia.com, *Observer Research Foundation*, New Delhi.

38. Rajat Pandit, "Chinese Airbases in Tibet," Times of India. Indiatimes.com, 08 March 2011.

39. Office of the Secretary of Defence USA, Annual Report to Congress, May 2012 and Dennis Blasko, The Chinese Army Today: Tradition and Transformation for 21st century, *Routledge*, UK, pp 87-102.

40. Military Balance, International Institute of Strategic Studies, London, Chapter on Asia, 2012.

41. Manoj Joshi, "Xi Jinping and PLA Reform", *Observer Research Foundation*, Occasional Paper, New Delhi, 2016, pp.19-29.

42. Richard Fisher, "China announces new theatre commands-Images", IHS Janes 360 at www.janes.com>article>china-announ..., February 2016.

*

CHAPTER 4

Chinese Defence Industrial Complex

Introduction

China has a long history of arms production, but it was only when the Communist Party came to power that attempts were made to develop a rational defence industry. The Soviet Union provided tremendous assistance in the 1950s when numerous factories were established to enable licensed production of Soviet weapons. By 1959, these plants were producing many weapons including jet aircraft. The aid abruptly ended in 1960 and the Chinese were left to fend for themselves.

The elementary defence industrial base in China was badly disrupted by the civil war and the Japanese invasion. The PLA had been reduced to a pitiful strength of just 10,000 at the end of the Long March. The Japanese invasion gave it a major reprieve as both the Communists and the Kuomintang (KMT) decided to put on hold the bitter civil war and fight the common enemy. By 1945, when the war got over, the PLA had grown to a strength of over 950,000. It expanded rapidly thereafter and undertook massive campaigns that involved 500,000 to 700,000 troops. It grew in size to almost 4.5 million men by the close of the civil war and the commencement of the Korean War. It then had an assortment of weapons and ammunition—American, Russian, Japanese and those captured from the KMT. Mao frantically asked the Soviets for military equipment to enable the PLA to take on the high-tech Americans and match them in firepower. Stalin was initially hesitant and Mao launched the Korean offensive without waiting for Soviet weapons. The fact is that the PLA was extremely nervous about facing a professional US Army without a transfusion of Soviet weapons and the Chinese had to work on their men for almost three months before they were psychologically primed to fight the US. The early Chinese successes, however, prompted Stalin to sell weapons to the Chinese Communists in huge quantities.

The Soviets, in fact, helped the Chinese to establish a fairly modern arms manufacturing base during the Korean War 41. In all, 156 key Soviet projects were set up for weapons production. The war-fighting abilities of the PLA impressed Stalin and he decided to arm China against the Americans in Korea. Following the setback of the Great Leap Forward in the late 1950s, the PLA's National Defense Science & Technology Commission (NDSTC) and the State Council of National Defence Industries Office (NDIO) combined to set up a joint system of R&D supervision and coordination amongst certain machine building industries. Surprisingly, this survived the consternation caused by the Cultural Revolution. The ideological conflict with the Soviet Union had led to a total withdrawal of Soviet technicians and engineers towards the end of the 1950s, causing a great setback for China's defence industry. It took the Chinese almost a decade to reverse engineer the Russian MiG-17 and MiG-19 fighters and T-series tanks.

Location of the Defence Industry

Mao was seriously concerned about a military invasion of China by the USA first and thereafter by the USSR. Like the Soviets had done in World War II, Mao now physically relocated his defence industries to the mountains, deep in China's heartland in the 1960s and 1970s, so that they would be safe from US air and sea-based attacks as also a land invasion by the Soviets. This seriously disrupted the functioning of the Chinese defence industry. The relocation was completed by about 1970. These areas lacked the requisite economic and transportation infrastructure and backup linkages with the civilian industry of the cities and coastal areas. Here they were in a standalone mode in backward districts where the quality of life for the staff and workers was quite low. China had to spend huge sums on recreating the basic and support infrastructure. In fact, estimates are that the Chinese spent some 50 per cent of their national investment to recreate this infrastructure. The defence industries incurred huge deficits. Some 55 per cent of Chinese defence industries are in these remote areas and this has seriously affected the efficiency of the Chinese military industrial complex.

Deng Xiaoping Era

Deng Xiao Ping had a clear vision for China. He logically visualised that there were no credible threats of a major land invasion of China either by the USA or the USSR. The threat was confined now to local or limited wars. As such he began a long-term program of the four modernisations. The first was agricultural and attained food sufficiency by providing private plots to farmers in State Collective Farms. Next came economic modernisation by liberalising and inviting hand me down technologies from the West. China soon became the world's workshop for low-end manufacture and most western firms moved their production plants to China to take advantage of its cheap labour force.

Chinese leaders had very closely studied the rise and fall of Nazi Germany. They were convinced that Germany had gone to war prematurely before consolidating its economic base. The Chinese very deliberately put economic modernisation above military modernisation. Further, they sought a peaceful periphery for China, in which it could carry out its economic modernisation in a peaceful and unhindered manner. The Chinese put off their military modernisation and focused on building their economic and science and technology base. For two decades the Chinese economy grew at an almost unprecedented ten percent per annum. The Chinese military industrial capacity was also diverted towards producing consumer goods and contributing to the economic build up. The PLA was told to wait patiently while this economic modernisation was completed. In fact in this period, only up to some ten per cent of the capacity of most defence units was utilised for producing weapons and equipment. Bulk capacity was diverted towards earning profits via consumer goods production.

Gulf War—A Wake-Up Call

The Gulf War of 1990 was a wakeup call for the Chinese. They were amazed at the technology demonstrated by the US military and the inability of Iraq with its Soviet weaponry to stand up and fight. Certainly, the PLA with its objectives on Taiwan and the South China Sea would face an uphill task without modernising its forces. This led to rapid discussions between various organs of the party and the first task was to reshape research and defence facilities.

Accordingly, it was deliberated to form a single body which could develop the Chinese defence industrial complex. The most important single body overseeing this is COSTIND, which was established in 1982. It combined the NDSTC, the NDIO and the Science & Technology Equipment

Commission of the CMC. The COSTIND served as a link to coordinate R&D and production. Over the years this system has encountered functional problems. Hence in March 1998, a new organisation was established. Under it was the General Armament Department (GAD) of the PLA and the State Administration of Science Technology and Industry for National Defence (SATSTIND). This replaced COSTIND. There are seven key institutions of higher learning under these organisations:

- Beijing University of Aeronautics;
- North West Polytechnic University;
- Nanjing University of Aeronautics & Astronautics;
- Harbin Institute of Technology;
- Beijing University of Science & Technology;
- Nanjing University of Science & Technology;
- Harbin Engineering University.

These higher learning institutions train talent for China's defence industries. Further, the modernisation of the Chinese defence industry has resulted due to four main factors. First of all, adequate funds have been made available by the government for defence acquisition. The second relates to a spin on benefits from the civilian economy. The third aspect relates to the integration of the Chinese defence industry with a global research and production chain which provides access to foreign technology, know-how and capital. The fourth relates to fundamental reforms building on the four mechanisms of competition, evaluation, supervision and encouragement. These factors provide a framework for assessing the effectiveness of reforms and the extent to which they are enabling China to strengthen its indigenous capabilities. The foundation of this framework is based on the principle of 'Yujun Yumin' (Locating Military Potential in Civilian Capability). This was put forward in the Sixteenth Party Congress in 2003.[1]

Prior to this, the Chinese tried to optimise their existing defence industry to produce civilian goods. The experiment was partially successful and resulted in the production of substandard goods in a few cases. There was a need to reform the State Owned Enterprises (SOE) which numbered around 305,000 and employed 109 million workers as they were not able to meet user requirements.[2] Meanwhile, various constituents of the PLA got actively involved in a variety of enterprises for raising funds for modernisation. It has been estimated that there have been as many as 20000 PLA-owned enterprises, including world-class hotels, transnational corporations and a large logistics industry. In July 1998, the PLA was officially banned from commercial activities, causing it immense pain. But it resulted in improvement of the defence industry.[3]

It is pertinent to note that China is still playing catch-up with regard to weapons technology. Progress notwithstanding, there are still issues which need further improvement. The statement of the Head of PLA's General Armaments Department (GAD) at the Sixteenth Party Congress in 2003 was, "There has been a marked improvement in national defence scientific research and in the building of weapons and equipment. The past five years has been the best period of development in the country's history."

There is no doubt that China's defence industry is on an upward curve. It may be pertinent to note that in January 2016, the former GAD was bifurcated into two departments, the first being the Equipment Development Department which will perform research, development, testing and evaluation (RDT&E) functions and will oversee procurement, management and information systems, building for the armed forces. However, the GAD's Science and Technology Commission which has been a nexus of civil-military cooperation on defence technological issues will not migrate to the Equipment Development Department and is placed directly under the Central Military Commission.

It is of interest to note what constitutes the Chinese defence industry. Basically, there are eleven important enterprises. These enterprises cover general areas of nuclear affairs, aerospace, aviation, shipbuilding, ordnance and electronics. These companies are as enumerated:

- China National Nuclear Corporation;
- China Nuclear Engineering Construction Corporation;
- China Aerospace Science and Industry Group Corporation;
- China Aerospace Science and Technology Group Corporation;
- China Aviation Industry Group Corporation I;
- China Aviation Industry Group Corporation II;
- China State Shipbuilding Corporation;
- China Shipbuilding Industry Corporation;
- China's North Industries Group Corporation;

- China South Industries Group Corporation;
- China Electronics Technology Corporation.

The creation of the erstwhile General Armament Department (GAD) in 1998 had made the distinction between purchaser (GAD) and the supplier (COSTIND). Via this mechanism, the market competition mechanism had been introduced into China's military industrial complex. The military industry has now been streamlined. Built earlier on the highly centralised Soviet model, which completely segregated the civil and military industries, China is now trying to integrate the two. China was placed under military technology sanctions after the 1989 Tiananmen Square incident. As such China tried to obtain dual-use technology via the civil sector and to ensure that defence R&D benefited the commercial/civilian sector. These backward and forward linkages of the defence and civilian industrial sector were imperative for overall and balanced growth. With American and European sanctions in place, China increasingly began to look towards Russia and Israel to gain the cutting edge technology. The Russian link has been invaluable. The Russians initially gave 4 x diesel-electric kilo submarines; 2 x Sovremenny class anti-surface missile destroyers; sold 50 x SU-27 fighters and permitted licensed production of some 200. The Chinese reverse-engineered these to produce the J-11 fighter. The Chinese took Israeli help to exploit the basic Lavi design to create the J-10—the F-16 equivalent, the mainstay of their fighter fleet. They produced a cheaper version using the MiG-29 engines called the JF-17. The Russians were alarmed at this reverse-engineering and violation of intellectual property rights and slowed down further sales to China. Italy has been helping with avionics and shipboard systems.

Current Status

The current status dates back to 2008. After the first plenary session of the Eleventh National People's Congress in 2008, the Chinese government created a new ministry, the Ministry of Industry and Information Technology, popularly known as MIIT. This ministry assumed functions over several government departments. These included the National Development Reforms Commission, SATSIND, the former Ministry of Information Industries and the State Council Information Office. The changes have brought about the synergy between the government and the defence industry. Further specific interests of the PLA are taken care of by the GAD. Though as per the latest reforms the GAD has been transformed into the Equipment Development Department and the Science and Technology Commission, it is important that the erstwhile organisation be researched to logically arrive at appropriate deductions. The erstwhile GAD which commenced its role in 1998 is the leading organ responsible for the policy-making and supervision of weapon design, development, production, procurement, maintenance and the life cycle management across all services in the PLA. Further, the new organisation currently manages China's space and nuclear weapons programme. It has also consolidated control over Defence R&D. It was formed by merging few branches from the General Staff Department, the General Logistics Department and COSTIND. The MIIT has control over SATSIND and the Defence Industrial Complex. SATSIND focuses solely on industrial planning and regulatory aspects of the defence industrial base.

The Chinese defence industrial complex, therefore, is dominated today by 11 SOEs that own hundreds of subsidiaries and together employ some two million workers. Primaries and affiliates are supported by thousands of third and fourth level/tier companies that provide sub-contracting services. In 2009, the state-owned enterprises posted revenues estimated at US $ 118 billion and boasted profits of about US $ 12 billion. This is indeed a positive step towards manufacturing state-of-the-art weaponry. These profits are an indicator that defence modernisation is leading China to economic growth by selling defence products to numerous countries. It would merit importance to view developments in two spheres—aerospace and shipbuilding.

The China Aviation Industry Corporation is currently the most profitable group posting US $ 15 billion in profits. These figures represent a considerable improvement over the losses reported in the 1990s. This was formed by the merger of two corporations in 2008 to make a giant entity that could compete with western multinationals like Lockheed Martin on a global scale. In 2009, the industry signed agreements with Chinese banks to procure loans worth over US $ 60 billion, over the next ten years. The group registered a number of its subsidiaries on the Chinese and global stock exchanges and issued bonds worth US $ 2.9 billion in 2009 for the first time. It includes over 200 trading companies and 30 research institutions.

Currently, the group employs 500,000 workers of which some 200,000 are engineers. It makes the Chengdu J-10 multi-role fighter (which is the equivalent of US F-16) and is the mainstay of the PLAAF Fighter Fleet. These are manufactured at Chinese aircraft institutes and branch companies. In addition, it has over forty ventures and six worker companies in the open coastal cities and Special Economic Zone (SEZs). The group also makes its cheaper version the JF-17 which it is jointly producing with Pakistan. Additionally, it makes the Shenyang J-11B and the Chinese derivative J-11A, which are both copies of the Russian SU-27SK. They also make the KJ-2000 Air-borne Warning and Control (AWAC) aircraft as also various UAVs. Some 50 J-10 have been delivered and the overall requirement will be 300. It will replace the J-6 and J-7 (MiG-19 and MiG-21 variants). Ultimate requirements will depend on how soon the J-20 and the J-31 Fifth Generation Fighter Aircraft are developed. The group has benefited greatly from increasing links between Chinese defence enterprises and commercial and military activities. Development of dual-use technologies and an industrial base that serves both military and civilian needs is amongst the highest priorities of the Chinese leadership. The group has acquired ten firms (Nine Chinese companies and the Australia-based Fischer Advanced Composites Components). This is its first overseas acquisition. Defence industry links to commercial economies are designed to facilitate the flow of technologies, know-how and investment in the defence enterprise often through a subsidiary. Once you are connected to civil aviation the military aspects gradually flow in.

China's State Ship Building Corporation and China's Ship Building Industry Corporation are two giant enterprises. These were given some US $ 38 billion worth of loans by Chinese banks in 2009. They employ about 350,000 workers. They own more than 60 affiliate companies. They have undertaken major modernisation and expansions in recent years with a focus on modular shipbuilding and technologies that facilitate construction across a number of subsidiaries.

China today is the third largest shipbuilder in the world and owns 40 percent of the world's merchant shipping tonnage. It is now building aircraft carriers, nuclear submarines, conventional submarines, Roll On Roll Off (RORO) ships, liquid petroleum gas carriers and high-speed hydrofoils. Ships built after 2000 were pre-fabricated and used modular construction techniques,

Figure 4.1: China's Nuclear Submarine[4]

which compare with the best in low-cost ship construction. The group is likely to build four to six aircraft carriers by the Jiangnan Shipyard Company at its Changxing Island shipyard.[5] Russian technologies and design influence most Chinese naval platforms, including aircraft carriers and now the Type 694 Jin class nuclear powered Ballistic Missile Submarine. Many shipbuilding technologies have been acquired through commercial partnerships with South Korea, Japan and some European countries. These have helped advance China's development of naval propulsion systems. China has left no stone unturned to acquire technologies from multifarious sources. China was in a catch-up mode and is currently moving on to Innovation. It is focusing on critical technologies which are as under:

- Nanotechnology,
- Robotics,
- Stealth,
- Artificial Intelligence,
- Biotechnology,
- Micro Optronics/Electronics,
- Cyber warfare,
- Radar and Microwave,
- State of the art Aerospace Technologies,
- Advanced Shipbuilding Technologies,
- Laser and Directed Energy Systems,

- Nuclear,
- Rocket and Missiles,
- Material Science,
- Micro Electro Mechanical Systems/Nano Electro Mechanical System,
- Combat Modeling and Simulation,
- Satellites,
- Information and Communication Technologies,
- Life Sciences,
- Geospatial Technologies,
- Big data,
- Quantum Communications.

Applications in these fields are elucidated in subsequent paragraphs.

Nanotechnology. Applications are to be done across a wide spectrum of equipment. The aspects to be dealt include conventional materials to be replaced by lighter, tougher and better alternatives. This could also result in camouflage through colour changes or intelligent surface coatings. The technology could play an important role in cyber warfare by miniaturising sensors, unobtrusive micro audio bugs and video recording devices and other electronic components. The powders and explosives could be miniaturised for use in propellants and explosives. Protective clothing for chemical biological radiological and nuclear which is currently cumbersome could be made flexible and user-friendly.

Robotics. The Chinese have been focusing on robotics in multifarious fields. They are being developed for clearance of minefields Improved Explosive Devices (IEDs) and breaching or clearance of obstacles. Further, they are being used as unmanned aerial, water, submerged and land vehicles. Logistically they have numerous applications to include ammunition handling and working in hazardous conditions. Stealth: The Chinese are incorporating stealth in their aircraft and ships. This enables avoiding detection by using technologies that reduce reflection of electromagnetic waves, visible light, radio frequency, infra-red and audio. China is working actively to develop stealth. China has made great strides in the field of UAV Swarms.

Artificial Intelligence. The Chinese are using Artificial Intelligence for all fields particularly with regard to computation, data analysis, neural networks, computer vision or virtual reality, image interpretation for target identification, missile trajectory analysis and identification friend or foe.

Biotechnology. The Chinese see biotechnology as assisting in advances especially in the fields of fuels, food, biotechnological weapons, Genetic weapons and biometrics to create materials, sensors and weapon systems based on biological principles.

Micro-Optronics, Electronics, Sensors. Imaging devices and range finders which would give 24x7 situation awareness. These would be mounted on surveillance and communication platforms and utilised in multimedia applications as also for networking.

Cyber Warfare. The Chinese have taken great strides in cyber warfare. They have focused on the following:

- Network intruder detection and prevention systems;
- Indigenous encryption/decryption technologies based on quantum computing;
- Electronic Warfare (EW) systems;
- Electro Magnetic Pulse bombs and other applications;
- Anti-IED equipment;
- Creation of indigenous operating systems;
- Indigenous manufacture of microprocessor chips.

Radar and Microwave. These have multifarious applications in the military domain. They are focusing on a variety of radars to include fire control, weapon locating, battle field surveillance, synthetic aperture, over the horizon and other states of the art systems.

Aerospace Technologies. China is in a catch-up mode to develop state-of-the-art technologies in these spheres. Like the US, China is developing two FGFAs for the PLAAF.

Shipbuilding Technologies. China is the third largest shipbuilder in the world. Its industries have refurbished an aircraft carrier, submarines, frigates, destroyers and numerous other vessels with current technology. Their research programmes will lead to more sophisticated development in the field of shipbuilding.

Laser and Directed Energy. These have multiple applications and are being used in target designation, range finding, early warning systems, directed energy weapon systems and missile defence.

Nuclear. This is being developed intensively. China has a tremendous advantage as they along with the US, France and Russia are among the four countries who build nuclear reactors. Military applications are being gainfully optimised in the armed forces. China is gradually using nuclear technology for its weaponry and propulsion of warships and submarines.

Rockets and Missiles. China has equipped its Second Artillery with an array of conventional and nuclear-tipped ballistic as also cruise missiles. The PLA has rocket regiments capable of firing up to more than 100 km. China has assisted Pakistan with this rocket technology to develop NASR which is used to fire tactical nuclear weapons. Asymmetric capability to attack targets anywhere on the globe is being attained through these rockets. China is also focusing on technology to counter rockets and missiles. Material Science. In conjunction with nanotechnology, another domain for development by China is in the field of material sciences. This could lead to better weapon systems, improved protective clothing and better materials.

Micro-Electrical Mechanical Systems/Nano-Electrical Mechanical Systems. This will be used in conjunction with other technologies to improve the quality of various weapon systems particularly with regard to components of sensors, seekers, accelerometers and components of gyros.

Combat Modelling and Simulation. The Chinese would like to train their forces at optimum costs. Training with combat modelling would provide for virtual reality and simulators would enable training in all skills needed by soldiers in the handling of equipment and devices.

Satellites. The GAD of the PLA is responsible for undertaking developments in outer space projects. China has focused on satellites for numerous military uses, including surveillance, reconnaissance and targeting. China has developed and tested Anti-Satellite (ASAT) weapons.

Information and Communication Technologies. The Chinese armed forces believe that secure and robust communications are only possible if engineered domestically. The focus is on software, hardware and networking architecture as also integrated platforms to support voice, data, video and multimedia. The PLA is leaving no stone unturned to undertake network centric warfare.

Life Sciences. The Chinese soldier must be capable of operating in all types of climate and terrain. They are focusing on remedies for high altitude sickness, integrated life support systems, nutritional packages for soldiers, bio-waste management, psychometric tests and psychotronic weapons. Further research is being undertaken in exoskeletons to enhance the ability of the soldiers.

Geospatial Technologies. The Chinese have focused intensely on this aspect and are developing their own navigation system called Beidou as also their indigenous Geo-Information System. This has enabled Jointness and interoperability in their forces.[6]

Big Data and Quantum Communications. China is a leader of Big Data and is competing with the US on quantum communications. On September 29, 2017, Chinese physicist Jian-Wei Pan laid the first long-distance online quantum communications, connecting Beijing and Shanghai. Quantum communications currently cannot be hacked and China is devoting a lot to this specialised field. China has been straining every sinew to acquire and absorb technologies by various means. They have acquired technology from foreign sources which have enabled them to expedite their numerous programmes. In July 2007, Federal Bureau of Investigation Director Robert Mueller remarked, "China is stealing our secrets in an effort to leap ahead in terms of its military technology. It is a substantial threat".[7] A few cases where the Chinese gathered information pertains to US nuclear warheads, F-117 stealth systems from an aircraft downed in Serbia, Northop Grumman's B-2 bomber, cruise, ballistic missile technology, sonar technology, Patriot Surface to Air Missile, and Anti-Submarine Technology. Currently, they have moved onto innovation.[8]

Chinese Reform of Military Industries

To push its military industries to the next stage of development, China has implemented two layered reforms in recent years. These include:

- Listing subsidiary companies of military corporations on the domestic and foreign stock exchanges. This will Consolidate and strengthen the industrial base. Further, provide access to finances from commercial markets that will boost R&D budgets. This will ensure long term sustenance and make Chinese companies market-driven entities that can compete at the global level.

• Measures to encourage consolidation of Chinese groups and the listing of their subsidiaries were commenced in 2007.

• Reforms aimed to achieve the best international practices so that they can move on from being domestic champions to international competitors.

As stated earlier, COSTIND has now been placed under the newly created MIIT and renamed as SATSIND. The primary roles of this new organisation are to nurture defence companies, formalise corporate practices and implement dual-use technology reforms. Thus China's defence industry has been almost entirely modelled on the erstwhile Soviet model. Today, the military industrial complex is producing numerous military platforms based on Russian and other technologies. The most high profile is the Shenyang J-11B, a license-produced version of the Russian SU-278K. The Chinese apparently have produced their variant J-11A by reverse engineering. However, the salient lesson learnt by the Chinese has been that the separation of the Soviet military and civilian industries prevented the osmosis of ideas and technology from one to the other. Russian military industries were highly competent but the Russian civilian industries got no spin-offs from the military R&D and production experience. The civilian sector of the Soviet economy lagged badly. The technology denial regime enforced after the Tiananmen Square incident of 1989 has impelled the Chinese to seek close linkages between their civilian and military industrial components.

Dual use technologies derived from military R&D and manufactured products have given the US civilian industry a major boost and enhanced its competitiveness. The Chinese reforms of their military-industrial sector are precisely trying to establish these linkages. The Chinese are thus trying to forge ahead of their Russian mentors. It is noteworthy that when the Soviet Union collapsed in 1990, India shopped desperately to get spare parts for its huge inventory of Soviet-era weapons. The Chinese, however, were body-shopping then for out of job Soviet designers, engineers and scientists. They hired them to refurbish their R&D base and indigenise their arms manufacturing sector in a far more effective manner than India has been able to achieve so far. Our indigenisation is confined to 30 per cent whereas the Chinese have now manufactured their entire fleet of 4th Generation jet fighters; are now sailing their own aircraft carriers, nuclear and conventional submarines, and making their own artillery, tanks, APCs and missiles along with their own family of small arms. They have very successfully exported these to Pakistan and other countries in South Asia, the Middle East, Iran, Africa and elsewhere. The Chinese military-industrial complex is now competing with the United States in terms of two Stealth FGFA models. Its most impressive strides have been in the realm of ballistic missiles and in its Dong Feng (DF) 21D, Aircraft Carrier Killer Missile with its associated satellite systems, may well have produced an asymmetric warfare system that could change the face of naval warfare. If the weapon system proves accurate in war, it would compel CBGs to move with Aegis Class Destroyers equipped with anti-ballistic missiles to destroy the DF-21D in flight preferably at the boost stage.

Assessment of Chinese Military Technology Capabilities

China's military industrial complex has enabled the PLA to modernise at a rapid pace. It would be of interest to note the technological capabilities of the Chinese armed forces. The US Department of Defence assessed critical military technologies involving 15 working groups, which reviewed more than 6000 technologies and identified 2060 as significant militarily. Out of these 656 met the critical criteria. Further, these were categorised into 18 critical technology areas for development and production of superior weapons. It is pertinent to note that 84 production elements were necessary for developing these areas.[9] The deductions are interesting to note. China has made a significant development in practically all technologies. Critical areas where China needs to catch up are mentioned below.

Space Systems. China is likely to catch up with the US to launch vehicle technology. However, in propulsion and power systems, it is lagging behind the USA by about ten years.

Navigation. China has launched its Beidou Satellite System. A report by Kevin

McCauley of The Jamestown Foundation on August 22, 2014, states the development of a fourth-generation satellite positioning chip which is expected to provide an accuracy of 2.5 metres for usage with the military and police. China began the construction of the Beidou System in 1994. In the first stage, up to 2007, four experimental satellites were launched into orbit. In 2003, preliminary trials were conducted. The second stage to provide regional coverage began in 2007. This covered the Asia Pacific region. Full operational capability for this system was reached on December 27, 2012. The third stage is to be operationalised with 35 satellites. China purchased 20 atomic clocks from Switzerland to assist the current programme. Currently, Russia has agreed to cooperate with China in this field and examine the feasibility of linking GLONASS with Beidou System. Currently, the PLA still relies on the GPS, but it is expected that within a decade the Chinese navigation system will have stabilised. Thus China has to develop further systems to have a totally indigenous navigation system. Sensors and Surveillance: In the field of digital real-time data collection, state-of-the-art surveillance and providing an integrated C^4I^2SR system, China is about 15 years behind the US.

Directed and Kinetic Energy Weapons. China has demonstrated an ASAT weapon in 2007. It is developing direct energy weapons under the Assassins Mace programmes but is currently at least 10 to 15 years behind the US.[10]

Reforms Undertaken by President Xi Jinping

The recent reforms being implemented by President Xi Jinping would see theoretical and technical innovation in the Chinese defence industry. There have been changes in the various departments under the new CMC. The General Armament Department has been substituted by the Equipment Development Department and all research and development would be under the Science and Technology Commission. These are likely to be undertaken gradually. By and large, the technological process would continue in the same direction.

Figure 4.2: Chinese Beidou Navigation System[11]

Analysis

Issues which merit consideration are enumerated below:

- China is aware of its lack of requisite technologies. Much as it would like to follow the classical path, it would like to inject speed by acquiring technologies through reverse engineering or by receiving inputs at high cost from Russia and if required steal from unauthorised sources. With increased awareness, they are now moving to the innovation stage. It is nice to note that India is also straining every sinew to improve its technology.

- Currently, the Chinese defence industry has become far more productive than in the past decades. The defence industrial reforms implemented after the First Gulf War were substantial and have positively influenced the quality of China's defence industrial output. Chinese defence firms have improved their R&D techniques, production processes and the quality of output. China is currently an exporter of defence weaponry. Currently, China's defence industry comprises of 11 state-owned enterprises.

- These firms cover the areas of nuclear affairs, aerospace, aviation, shipbuilding, ordnance and electronics. All of these firms are under the MIIT and assisted by SATSIND. Since the early 1980s, Deng Xiaoping had directed China's defence industrial firms to diversify away from exclusive military production to producing civilian goods for domestic and international markets Current estimates of the amount of civilian production in each of the eleven large defence corporations range from 65 per cent to 90 per cent depending on the firm's capabilities. Further, with the formation of MIIT which includes SATSIND, the Equipment Development Department and the Science and Technology Commission of the PLA assumed the responsibilities of procurement for weapons, including issues involving Outer Space.[12]

- Further, the government has also provided incentives for efficiency and innovation. The government has kept away from enterprise operations which have enabled them to become more market-oriented by exposing them to the pressure of competition, subjecting them to budgetary constraints, removing practically state subsidies and make them overall self-sustaining. Currently, most industries have favourable balance sheets. These reforms have led to a leaner and more capable defence industry in China.

- The output of the current defence industrial complex has assisted China's military modernisation considerably. China today is capable of orchestrating military operations in all five domains of warfare which pertain to land, sea, air, cyber and outer space. China's shipbuilding industry is building aircraft carriers, destroyers and submarines. It's aerospace industry is developing two FGFAs, satellites and all variants of ballistic and cruise missiles. The modern capabilities of China's defence electronics and information technology sectors have facilitated the modernisation of the PLA's C^4I^2SR system. Currently, the PLA continues to build an infrastructure that is increasingly digital, automated, encrypted, faster, secure and wider in terms of bandwidth.

- These improvements in China's defence industrial capabilities have ensured that most companies are sailing on an even keel. Many of the classic structural weakness have been removed and a few of them have become efficient, innovative and profitable. The best performance has been by two aerospace conglomerates and the two shipbuilding conglomerates. China's defence industries are increasingly playing a pivotal role in the future direction and military competence of the PLA. Though they have a reasonable distance to catch up, they are innovating rapidly to develop and manufacture state-of-the-art defence equipment. The Chinese defence industry is unique and different from similar industries in the US, Russia, Japan and South Korea.

The overall indigenisation of the Chinese defence industry has resulted in a transformation of the country from a defence importer to an exporter. Apart from Pakistan, Sri Lanka is expected to buy the JF-17 jet fighter and Bangladesh is procuring submarines. The sale of defence products gives China a superior status which makes it more assertive in its dealings. This has also resulted in Chinese submarines berthing in Sri Lanka as also in acquiring control over the port of Gwadar in Pakistan. This has enabled the Chinese Navy to gradually posture in the Indian Ocean, thereby posing a threat to India. The recent reforms by President Xi Jinping would further enhance Chinese defence industrial capability.[13]

India through its current Make in India initiative is practically on the same frequency as China. We have made excellent progress in missiles and are today focusing on aircraft carriers, nuclear submarines and other land-based systems. We are also focusing on Artificial Intelligence and other related technologies. India like China is developing its MIRV and Manoeuverable Reentry Vehicle (MARV) and is soon going to gradually test Agni VI which would be an ICBM. There is a minimal gap which we are doing our best to bridge by synergising research by the Defence Research and Development Organisation (DRDO), public sector units and the private sector.

NOTES

1. James Mulvenon and Rebecca Sam Tyroler, "China's Defence Industry on the path to reforms", US-China Economic and Security Review Commission, USA, October 2009, pp 5-10.
2. Air Commodore Ramesh Phadke, "China's Power Projection", Manas Publications, New Delhi, 2005, pp. 159-162.
3. James Mulvenon, "Soldiers of Fortune", M.E.Sharpe, New York, 2001, p.3.
4. "Aircraft Carriers", Sino Military,www.chnqiang.com/article/2009/0605/article 86104.shtml
5. M Yang and Hong Yu-2011, "China's Industrial Development in the 21st century", pp. 52-53 and Changxing Island Shipbuilding base.

6. Jeffery Lin and P W Singer, "First Picture of Chinese Secretive new Submarine",www.popsi.com/blogs, 23 June 2013.

7. Lieutenant General J S Bajwa, "Modernization of the Chinese PLA-from Massed Militia to Force projection", Centre for Land Warfare Studies, Lancer Publishers and Distributors, New Delhi, 2013, pp. 154-157.

8. "China's new spy chief, a specialist on US, Japan and Economic Espionage", East Asia Intel.com, 5 September 2007.

9. Richard D Fisher Jr, "China's Military Modernisation", Pentagon Press, New Delhi, pp 35-36.

10. Bernard D Cole and Paul H B Godwin, "Advanced Military Technology and the PLA: Priorities and Capabilities of the 21st century", Book Chinese Armed Forces in the 21st century, Edited by Larry Wortzel, December 1999, pp. 169-170.

11. Jeffery Lin and P W Singer, "China joins the Laser Arms Race", popsi.com/blogs, 30 July 2015.

12. Peter B. De Selding, "China's Official Beidou Gear will receive GPS, Glonass, Galileo signals", spacenews.com, 06 February 2015.

13. Evan S Medeiros, "Analysing China's Defence Industries and implications for Chinese Military Modernisation", RAND Corporation, 1700 Main Street, Santa Monica, California, USA, 2004, pp 2-11.

*

CHAPTER 5

An Assertive China and its Impact on Global Security

Introduction

A nation-state has to assert itself domestically and internationally for its day-to-day activities. Prior to the creation of the People's Republic of China, China's assertiveness existed for over 4500 years. The country's military history is filled with assertive actions by various dynasties. The Chinese were the first to invent gunpowder. The invention of gunpowder is usually attributed to Chinese alchemy and is popularly listed as one of the four great inventions of China. The invention was made as early as the Tang Dynasty (9th century), but certainly by the Song Dynasty (11th century). Further, China's assertiveness through the Mongol conquests of the 13th century resulted in the spread of knowledge of gunpowder. However, as early as 492 Chinese alchemists have noted that saltpeter burns with a purple flame allowing for practical efforts at purifying the substance which is one of the most important constituents of gunpowder.[1]

This assertive spirit continues in the development of rockets by China. The availability of gunpowder was a precursor to the development of the first solid rocket propellant. The first recorded use of rockets was in 1232 against the Mongols. One of the earliest texts in which the use of rockets has found a mention is the Huolongjing, written by the Chinese artillery officer Jiao Yu in the mid-14th century. The written text also mentions the first use of a multi-stage rocket, the Fire Dragon, which was used mostly by the Chinese Navy. It is pertinent to note that rocket technology reached the Europeans through Genghis Khan when he conquered parts of Russia and Europe. This assertiveness has continued to manifest itself in both domestic and international disputes.

Assertiveness: The Current Dispensation

China has enhanced its assertiveness ever since the People's Republic of China was established in 1949. Mao Zedong, the founder, clearly stated that "Power flows from the barrel of a Gun."[2] Immediately after its creation, China fought the Korean War which was followed by the war with India in 1962. Thereafter it secured the Paracel Islands from Vietnam in 1974 and fought a war with Vietnam in 1979. Deng Xiao Ping transformed China's outlook to the world and enhanced its comprehensive national power, resulting in the accession of Hong Kong and Macau from the United Kingdom and Portugal respectively. Currently, China has capabilities which permit it to exercise strategic options suiting its acquisition of the new Chinese dream which is based on strength and wealth. This rise in assertiveness has been witnessed particularly post-2008, when the US and other Western economies faced recession. Jess Miller in Rense.com attributes these to the authoritarian style of government with a modernised armed force and a current GDP of US $ 9.2 trillion with a growth rate of about 7.5 per cent. Further, the PLA continues to be an important player in the Chinese Communist Party and has been the backbone for Chinese infrastructure projects and, despite best efforts, continues to covertly run business and industry.

It is of interest to note that more than two decades after the end of the Cold War, conditioned by its geopolitical isolation, China has learned to adapt to US domination, following the 'Low Profile (Taoguang Yanghui)' policy set by Deng Xiao Ping. This policy was set when the Chinese armed forces embarked on a modernisation drive post the First Gulf War.[3] Currently, Chinese leaders are unwilling to make adjustments and have begun to assert Chinese interests. Chinese core interests can possibly be summarised by what State Councillor Dai Binguo told Americans at the first China-US Strategic and Economic Dialogue in July 2009. He stated that China's primary interest is to maintain its fundamental system and security. The next is state sovereignty and territorial integrity and finally stable development of the economy and society. The most important issue as per this statement is the survival of the current authoritarian system which could be threatened by domestic forces in combination with covert foreign forces. The second applies to the issues of Taiwan, Tibet, Ussuri River, Spratly and Paracel Islands. These are issues which directly impact external security. The third issue deals with economic stability which justifies the Chinese Communist Party's rule in China.

China has certainly been more assertive since 2008. The abrupt cancellation of the European Union summit due to former French President Nicholas Sarkozy meeting the Dalai Lama and the opposition of US arms sales to Taiwan as also President Barack Obama meeting the same Tibetan leader, resulted in China threatening to impose sanctions on American companies involved in arms sales. Thus, China which was always receiving sanctions, for the first time, reversed the swing.[4]

The new leadership under President Xi Jinping took charge in March 2013. He has been eloquent about the "Chinese Dream" which primarily focuses on two issues "Strength and Wealth". The PLA has played a prominent role in cementing the authority of the current establishment and the world soon witnessed incursions by the PLA in the Depsang Plains of Ladakh in April 2013, at Chumar in September 2014, followed by incursions in the disputed Japanese Senkaku Islands and the declaration of China's Air Defence Identification Zone (ADIZ), covering most of East China Sea in November 2013. China today is clear about its ambitions and is assisting North Korea and Pakistan in its nuclear weapons programme. Both countries are being used to threaten the US and India. It is supplying economic and military assistance to Nepal, Myanmar, Sri Lanka and Bangladesh, countries that are in India's neighbourhood. Further, it continues to logistically improve its position in the disputed islands of the South China Sea and the East China Sea. It has recently refused to implement the Permanent Court of Arbitration Ruling on the South China Sea. The Doklam intrusion by China in June 2017 was contested by India, and after 73 days, China finally withdrew on August 28, 2017.

Further, between November 9 and 12, 2013, the third plenum of the 18th Communist Party Congress took place in which the formation of a new National Security Commission was announced by the present leadership. Security considerations in China in the recent period are varied in nature and indicate their diversification in the military and non-military aspects. National security is of utmost importance to the country's leadership and encompasses both internal and external dimensions. President Xi Jinping was named the Chairman of the National Security Commission while Premier Li Keqiang and the speaker of the Parliament Zhang Deqiang were named as Vice Chairmen of the National Security Council. According to an official statement, the Committee will be making overall plans and coordinating major issues on national security. According to Senior Colonel Gong Fangbin of the National Defence University, the National Security Council will tackle five threats. These would include the following:

- Countering extremism;
- Ideological challenges posed by Western culture to the Chinese;
- Cyber security;
- Unconventional security threats;
- Other non-traditional security challenges.

While the CMC handles traditional security issues, the National Security Council tackles long-term security issues from its roots.[5] China's assertiveness is vindicated by this new security framework under President Xi Jinping. This new commission appears to be taking over some of the responsibilities already assigned to other organisations to enable enhancement of the command system as also the responsive mechanisms. The various security groups which the council controls are the Foreign Affairs Group, State Security Group, Overseas Propaganda Group, Taiwan Affairs Group, Hong Kong & Macao Affairs Group, Finance & Economics Group and the Energy Group. The formation of these groups led to a new clash of interests in the South China Sea which is again indicative of China's assertiveness. Details of the same are elucidated in succeeding paragraphs.

The Paracel Islands were occupied by Chinese from the erstwhile South Vietnamese in 1974. Ever since, China, has been spreading its influence over other islands in the South China Sea. It has built a small garrison town Sansha in the Woody Island of the Paracel Group. Sansha has an airport and a runway of 2700 metres which enables the Chinese Air Force to operate in the area.

The China National Off-shore Oil Company's decision to move an oil rig—HD-981—was a pre meditated move which has hurt Vietnam and other claimants of islands on the South China. The oil rig was escorted by about 80 ships of the People's Liberation Army Navy (PLAN) as also the Chinese Coast Guard and moved into the South China Sea on May 2, 2014. The rig remained in location for three months and drilling operations continued during this period. The commencement of drilling was formally opposed by the Vietnamese Deputy Prime Minister and Foreign Minister Pham Binh Minh who telephoned China's State Councillor Yang Jiechi indicating violation of the Law of Seas. China listened to the minister but continued the drilling process. Vietnam sent 35 ships out of which 29 were armed and the rest were fishing vessels. On May 4, 2014, Chinese ships rammed two Vietnamese Sea Guard vessels, injuring seven Vietnamese. Chinese ships with air support were also used to intimidate six more Vietnamese ships. Further water cannons were also used to threaten the Vietnamese. As of now not a single round has been fired.

Figure 5.1: Chinese Oil Rig in South China Sea[6]

The stand-off led to demonstrations in urban areas of Vietnam. There have been reports of Taiwanese factories being attacked who the Vietnamese were mistaking for Chinese. The situation remained heated till the rig was withdrawn. The moot point is why did China dispatch oil rig—HD-981—to the Paracel Islands? The rig had been positioned immediately after the visit of US President Obama to Japan, South Korea, Philippines and Malaysia. The Chinese military posturing with their navy and air force was possibly to test the US response to such an eventuality. The Chinese feel that the US is currently tied down with Iran, Syria, Iraq and Ukraine. They neither have their forces nor the inclination to get involved in matters relating to the South China Sea.

Possibly Vietnam too would be seeking military partnerships to strategically balance China's posturing. The incident points to China's recent assertiveness which has been enhanced during the tenure of President Xi Jinping. China has refused to implement the 2016 Permanent Court of Arbitration Ruling and continues to stabilise its position on the South China Sea.

The 19th National Congress of the CPC was held between 18 and 24 October 2017. Xi Jinping was elected leader for life and spoke for more than three hours. The gist of his speech was as under:

- China offers an alternative model to the world;
- China's soft power and international standing has risen like never before;
- Socialism with Chinese characteristics would be the factor in domestic issues;
- A World Class Military by 2050;
- World's second largest economy to keep doors open;
- Firm warnings to separatist forces in Taiwan and elsewhere;
- Fight against corruption will continue.

Impact on Global Security

The PLA is in the process of modernising. Its capability far exceeds its regional defensive needs and is on a trajectory to compete with the US to achieve Asian military dominance. This competition has already moved on to outer space and is gradually moving to additional strategic priority areas. Chinese leaders iterate that their build-up is defensive and poses no threat to international peace. China is gradually developing its military capabilities to fulfill its territorial ambitions. In order to achieve these objectives, it is focusing on developing a broader array of military capabilities that more specifically challenge those of the US in space, air, cyber, sea and land.

There are numerous threats posed globally by China's recent disposition. The first is its unwillingness to follow global conventions on the proliferation of missiles and nuclear weapons. In particular, China has given extensive nuclear weapon and missile technology to North Korea and Pakistan. Further, China also to a lesser extent assisted Iran in its nuclear weapons programme. It is indeed strange that despite China leading the six-party talks since 2004 continues to assist North Korea in its development of nuclear weapons. The second threat is the military occupation of Taiwan. The Chinese are still weak in air force as also in landing crafts to pump in at least three group armies preceded by a cyber and short range ballistic missile attack. The capture of Taiwan would also entail military involvement with the United States which current capability does not permit. They would find it difficult even with the current modernisation as the US remains an impediment. The third threat is the asymmetric capability to use cyber, ASAT and anti-ship ballistic missiles to prevent movement of troops into theatres of operation. This is often termed as the Anti-Access/Area Denial (A2/AD) strategy. Currently, the Air-Sea Battle Concept and the Rebalancing Pivot Strategy of the US precludes a Chinese advantage, but over a period of time, this could be a crucial issue. Recently, US Vice President Michael Pence told participants at the East Asia Summit in November 2018 that the US will support freedom of navigation in the South China Sea. China, in the meantime, continues to dominate Asian countries by trying to dictate the Code of Conduct to ASEAN and undertaking submarine probes in the Indian Ocean.

China's ability to pose asymmetric challenges will soon be joined by a growing ability to pose numerous conventional challenges. This is the fourth threat and could witness threats to Arunachal, islands in the South China Sea and East China Sea and other claimed areas of Outer Mongolia and the Ussuri River. The fifth and the final threat is the challenge to deterrence due to the reduction of forces of the US and other NATO countries. There is a serious need to reconsider the US downscaling of force levels in view of the Chinese modernisation coupled with ambitions. It would be pertinent to examine how the PLA is shaping up for power projection in the future.

Projecting Power Leading to Assertiveness

On September 21, 2014, President Xi Jinping, demonstrating China's assertiveness, asked his troops to improve their combat readiness and sharpen their ability to win a regional war in the Information Technology Age. The president also expressed his unhappiness with the military and underlined the need to improve military command efficiency under new circumstances.[7] China while professing peace is developing capabilities to project power through its modernised military.

In its 2006 Quadrennial Defence Review, the Department of Defense of US warned that China is developing a long-range power projection force that challenges the assessment that China was looking only at Taiwan and its other claims on its periphery. Presently, China's immediate aim is to be the leading power in Asia while it enhances its capabilities to be effective beyond the Asian continent. In 2005, Lieutenant General Liu Yazhou of the PLAAF told a reporter, "When a nation grows strong enough, it practices hegemony. The sole purpose of power is to pursue even greater power. The frontiers of our national interests are expanding. Our military strategy should embody characteristics of time."[8] Michael Pillsbury, a US defence analyst, states there are analysts in China who expect China to be the dominant power possibly by 2050.[9]

Effective projection of power is a sign of military assertiveness and China has been building these capabilities in exercises with Russia since 2005. The first exercise was held in 2005 at China's Shandong Peninsula. These exercises were conducted under the auspices of the Shanghai Cooperation Organisation. This exercise involved Russia sending airborne troops, Marines, Sukhoi-27 fighters and the TU-22M Backfire bomber. Further PLAN and Russian submarines and destroyers conducted exercises. These exercises were a learning experience for the Chinese as this was the first opportunity to test their modernised forces with a country who had recently undertaken combat operations in Chechnya. They conducted joint airborne troop drops, an amphibious beach assault, air defence and naval blockade missions. All these manoeuvres would be essential to capture Taiwan. A similar exercise was conducted in the Chelyabinsk region of Russia from August 9 to 17, 2007. The 2007 exercise did not involve naval forces and long-range bombers. The exercise entailed long-range deployments for airborne troops, light mechanised armour and air support elements. A similar exercise was undertaken in September 2016.

These exercises demonstrated military capabilities essential for China to play an assertive military role in world affairs. Senior Colonel Lu Chuang, chief of the command group for the exercises, noted that the force included one army task force, one air force task force and one integrated support task force. Lu further enunciated that the exercise would allow the PLA to test four key capabilities as stated below:

- Capability in long-distance mobility;
- Capability in joint operations;

- Capability in carrying out precision engagement;
- Capability in long distance integrated support.[10]

It would be pertinent to examine these aspects to understand the Chinese reach in undertaking operations. This particularly gains importance due to the recent declaration of ADIZ, movement of a mobile oil rig with ship and fighter jets escorts in the South China Sea as also transgressions across the LAC with India and Bhutan.

The first time that the PLA conducted a long distance mobilisation of land forces across a distance by train over 10300 km was in 2005. A force of about 1600 troops from the 31 Group Army of the Nanjing Military Region opposite Taiwan, 36 Group Army near Beijing and the 15 Airborne Army participated in this exercise. They were provided air support by 16 Haig WZ-9 attack helicopters plus 16 MI-17 transport helicopters. They also used the Light Airborne tank which was transported on the IL-76 aircraft. In early September 2014, China carried out six intensive exercises. An Air Defence Brigade of Chengdu MAC (now Western Command) conducted a transregional live ammunition drill. Fire 2014 involving 6 MACs was carried out in North, North East and North West China. The exercise involved more than 20,000 troops. Similar exercises have been regularly conducted in the Tibetan Autonomous Region. These exercises give greater confidence to the PLA in combating adversaries while staking their claims.

To be prepared for combat operations in the future joint operations are extremely important. The PLA used their air force only during the Korean War in 1950, and thereafter, all wars were fought exclusively by the army. There is no way in which the PLA will capture Taiwan or fight its future operations through the singular application of its forces. Accordingly, China can be assertive only if its application of force is combined to maximise its combat potential on its adversary. This is an area which concerns leaders at the highest level. The third Plenary Session of the 18th Communist Party Central Committee Meeting held on November 16, 2013 discussed establishing the creation of theatre commands to synergise the functioning of Chinese combat power. The Chinese Ministry of National Defence has stated the need for establishing a joint operations command system to meet the requirements of modern warfare. A Xinhua report of January 6, 2014 stated that a statement was published on China Military Online on November 29, 2013 in which it was brought out that the PLA was conducting research into a joint operations command system with Chinese characteristics. Further, the National Defence University book strongly argued for the creation of joint operations command for future operations.

The Joint Command established by the PLA following reforms introduced by President Xi Jinping suggests a flatter unified command which will be a system of systems organisation encompassing all aspects, including C^4I^2SR. The PLA views the integration of joint forces down to the tactical level as an important joint operations requirement which will significantly synergise application of force in an optimised manner. Further forces will be formed at the strategic and campaign level. Ongoing debates within the PLA and in academic circles and limited current joint capabilities indicate that development of an integrated joint capability along with support operations capability will take possibly a decade. By 2030, it would be a fully integrated force capable of having a joint structure in terms of theatre commands capable of dealing with situations comprehensively.[11] Reforms of February 2016 highlight this aspect. This can be questioned as such reforms would take a longer time to be fine-tuned and may be realised by 2040.

The next aspect deals with precision engagement. Ever since the First Gulf War, China has been keen to undertake precision engagements. These have seen the development of laser bombs as also guided weaponry for the navy and ground forces. It may be pertinent to note that if there is a great power war in this century, it will not begin with the sound of explosions on the ground and in the sky but rather with the bursting of kinetic energy and flashing of laser light in the silence of outer space. China is engaged in an Anti-Satellite (ASAT) weapons drive that has profound implications for further military strategy in the Pacific. The PLA has been developing ASAT weapons since the 1990s. The Pentagon first publicly disclosed that China was developing a direct ascent ASAT missile in its annual report on Chinese military power in 2003. The report also pointed out that this type of ASAT system was only one part of a larger spectrum of offensive capabilities aimed at vitiating US dominance in space.[12] It was not long before the US Department of Defense report was proven correct. Beginning in September 2004, the PLA reportedly began a series of three direct ascent ASAT tests, which led up to the fourth, this time successful test that destroyed the FY-1C weather satellite on January

11, 2007.[13] These ASAT missiles pose a serious challenge to satellites that operate in Low Earth Orbit. These satellites provide photographic, electro optical, synthetic aperture radar and electronic intelligence. Loss of these satellites would be a serious blow to any nation prior to the start of a campaign. The destruction of the weather satellite in 2007 again demonstrates China's assertiveness where it could seriously impact satellites in low earth orbits which assist surveillance, reconnaissance, target acquisition and engagement.

To facilitate precision engagement, China has been devoting significant resources to directed energy weapons systems, particularly and have them to target satellites. According to one account the Chinese routinely turn powerful lasers skywards, demonstrating their potential to dazzle or permanently blind low earth orbiting satellites while they are passing over China.[14] Further, China's development of Anti-Ship Ballistic Missile (ASBM) capability is driven by the necessity to create conditions necessary for the resolution of differences with Taiwan on terms favourable to China. China's growing arsenal of increasingly accurate and lethal ballistic missiles already poses significant challenges to fixed targets on Taiwan, Okinawa and areas in India opposite Tibet. Upgrades have enabled them to engage maritime targets. Chinese writings indicate a near term requirement to keep US CBGs at a distance of at least 2000 km from China's eastern coastline. As quoted in a prominent journal, "The initiative is essential against an aircraft carrier battle group. That is when a large and powerful aircraft carrier battle group is coming to intervene; we must take the initiative and attack it. We must destroy it or drive it back beyond 2000-3000 km or more from the shoreline and not allow it to approach closer. The offensive action is essential because evasion and concealment is useless under the eyes of hundreds of satellites and in the face of the hundreds of Tomahawk Cruise Missiles with the range of thousands of km which every aircraft battle group has. Trying to hide means only passively taking a beating. If we hope to win this war, we must attack and repel the big and powerful aircraft carrier battle group beyond our gates."[15] In addition to the missile system which currently is based on the DF-21D, Chinese R&D appears to be focused on the means to maintain a persistent track of maritime targets of interest. These would include space based remote sensing assets, over the horizon sky wave radar systems and UAVs. These would provide data to the Joint Theatre Command as well as Second Artillery's operational level command centre.

To be assertive, China finally needs the capability in long distance integrated support. Logistic support is an important asset of power projection. For the exercises held in 2007, Senior Colonel Lu indicated that this aspect included communications, equipment, meteorology and logistics which are indispensable for any manoeuvre. The fine-tuning of these aspects will determine the success of any operation. As a matter of fact, joint logistic support will be a key to undertake any operation by the PLA.[16] The PLA is also building its capability to project by sea and by air.

The General Logistics Department (GLD) is the apex body providing logistics support to the three services and Second Artillery. It has sub-departments which manage a wide range of support services, including supplies, transportation, military communications, financial affairs, health, petroleum, oil and lubricants, economic production, barracks and capital construction. The GLD also oversees the PLA's efforts to grow much of its own food, production of clothing equipment and consumable items. In 2000, the Logistics Department of the seven Military Regions was reorganised into Joint Logistics Department (JLD). This was the first step in integrating logistics of the Military Regions. Under the joint logistics scheme, Air Force and Naval fleet transferred their general logistics support elements common to all services such as hospitals, fuel and motor vehicle maintenance to the MR JLD while keeping specialised logistics support elements unique to their own service. About 30 logistics sub-departments are subordinate to the MR, each consisting of hospitals, warehouses, depots and transportation units. Logistics sub-departments form mobile support units to accompany combat forces in the field or at sea, away from their bases. As part of reforms in the PLA reserve units, each MR has established a Reserve Logistics Support Brigade. In the reformed system, the system is known as the Joint Logistic Support Force with similar characteristics.

The GLD, through the JLD of MR (Theatre Commands), manages approximately 80 percent of logistic needs. The Logistics Departments of the four services manage the remaining 20 percent of the requirement. The JLD is subdivided into regional logistics support which manages material and services within the MR. The GLD has direct control over a number of supply units and strategic support bases around the country which provide general logistics support. The JLD has achieved considerable interface with National Logistics Infrastructure.

The future logistics philosophy which has commenced implementation focuses on quality vis-a-vis quantity. The essential characteristics are as under:

- Unified joint logistics to overcome compartmentalisation among the services;
- Light and modular logistics system compatible with mobile operations by Rapid Response formations;
- Integration and utilisation of civil transport and infrastructure;
- Emphasis on Just in Time Logistics as part of Precision Logistics;
- Integrated Technical Support for field formations and Communication Zones;
- Application of scientific methods in management of logistics;
- Increasing outsourcing for better utilisation of combat resources.[17]

The PLA currently practices mobilisation using civil transport. In a few years, China would have enough landing craft and logistic facilities to launch operations against Taiwan. It has built an excellent logistics infrastructure against Tibet. Further logistics for the RRF and the missile forces have increased exponentially.[18] Having viewed the assertiveness on projection pertinent to land, it is important to assess airmobile and maritime capabilities.

For any nation to be assertive it must have the capability to project power. China has been focusing on airmobile capabilities since 2007. Initially, the capabilities were confined to about 25 to 40 Shaanxi Y-8 medium transports, copies of the Ukranian Anotov AN-12 and about 20 Russian IL-76. China is currently developing a large transport aircraft. The project was to be completed by 2015 with a possible induction by 2020. Due to delays, the first prototype is likely to be ready by 2018. The aircraft would be known as the Y-20. The Y-20 as per Tang Changhong, Chief Designer, states that it will be a heavy duty aircraft having maximum takeoff weight and altitude. It is reported that the maximum takeoff weight would be 220 tons and the payload will be 66 tons. The most difficult component is the engine. The Chinese state that its creation is proceeding smoothly. The new transport aircraft, which has similarities to the C-17 Globe Master, will enable Chinese medium armour to be airlifted to suitable areas, thereby giving them capability for global manoeuvre.[19]

China's efforts to improve its ability to project maritime military power are of great interest to littoral countries in Asia and other important maritime powers. For China, building maritime projection capabilities is not just an issue of defence, it is also perceived through the lens of nationalism. It indicates the Chinese resolve to reverse the humiliation of the era of Western and Japanese dominance while asserting China's claim to regional leadership. It is difficult to estimate China's maritime power ambitions. However, it is possible to explore China's progress in three areas; aircraft carriers, amphibious projection and non-nuclear cruise missiles to be delivered by nuclear submarines. These provide the Chinese the right to intervene in other countries to protect Chinese interests. Carrier and amphibious forces also allow for the projection of China as a soft power, be it through a show of force, high profile exercises with allies, or participation in peacekeeping and humanitarian missions.

The first part is the aircraft carrier which China has inducted into the Chinese Navy. Admiral Liu Huaqing, a senior PLAN officer and proponent of naval modernisation, has spoken of the 21st century as the century of the sea. He has called for modernisation over several decades.[20] The PLAN had expressed an interest in operating an aircraft carrier around 1970, in consonance with its blue water operations. In 2011, PLA Chief of General Staff Chen Bingde confirmed that China was constructing at least one aircraft carrier. On September 25, 2012, China's first aircraft carrier "Liaoning" was commissioned. The process of construction involved acquiring four retired aircraft carriers for study, the Australian HMAS Melbourne and the erstwhile Soviet carriers Minsk, Kiev and Varyag. The design as also the landing systems were all obtained from Russia. China has also constructed its own carrier-based aircraft, the J 15. US Defense Secretary Chuck Hagel visited the carrier on April 7, 2014. Liaoning can carry 30 J-15 aircraft (the equivalent of Sukhoi-33). The fighter is still on the trial phase and on November 25, 2012, two aircraft landed on the aircraft carrier. According to the Shanghai Morning Post, China's first aircraft carrier will carry 24 J-15, four Z-18J early warning helicopters, six Z-18F anti-submarine helicopter and two Z-9C search and rescue helicopters. PLAN Senior Colonel Weidong a Research Fellow at the Navy Military Academy Research Institute, has stated that the aircraft carrier has the capability to undertake its tasks, thereby achieving sea and air dominance. The ship also carries a variety of missile systems.[21] By 2030, China will definitely aim for at least three aircraft carriers and possibly have one of these propelled by nuclear energy. Reports indicate they may go in for four to six aircraft carriers. However, it takes about 20 years to master the subtleties of the Carrier and, in this field, even India has an advantage.

Another important aspect in maritime assertiveness is through the Amphibious Projection Forces. The launching of the Landing Platform Dock, Type 071, by the Hudong Zhonghua Shipyard in Shanghai in December 2006, heralded a new capability for the PLA with regard to amphibious warfare. Ships such as these carry troops with their associated armour, artillery, transport and attack helicopters. Equipped with modern hovercrafts, the Landing Platform Dock enables naval landing operations to commence far from the coastline, enabling smooth operations on the beach head. These ships would assist the PLA in its likely task of undertaking operations against Taiwan. Jane's Fighting Ships 2014-2015 states that the first three ships in the class were commissioned in 2007, 2011 and 2012. The Type 071 design has an estimated displacement of more than 18,500 tons. It is estimated that the ship is likely to carry two hovercrafts, 500 to 800 troops plus about 25 to 50 combat vehicles. The ship would approximately carry 25 landing ship tanks. Further, each Type 071 can accommodate two Changhe Z-8 size helicopters. These can carry thirty armed troops as well as 4000 kg of cargo internally. The Type 071 can also carry the WZ-10 attack helicopters. The numbers of Type 071 held by the PLA are not known but there would be a sizeable requirement to launch operations against Taiwan.

As per an Asian Defence News report dated April 16, 2014, China is constructing its first Landing Helicopter Dock Type 081. The ship is likely to weigh about 20,000 tons and can embark eight helicopters with hangar space for four. Endurance is 25 to 30 days at sea with accommodation for 1068 Marines.[22] There are reports that China would be building six such crafts. China could build nine Type 071 and these in conjunction with six Type 081 could see about 8000 troops for short range missions against Taiwan. The number would be reduced for missions in the East China Sea and the South China Sea. By 2030, the Chinese PLAN would be making forays into the Bay of Bengal and the Indian Ocean, asserting their power to protect their lines of communication through the Straits of Malacca and the Sunda Straits. Certainly, the force level for amphibious power projection is smaller than the United

States which has 13 Landing Helicopter Docks and 24 Landing Platform Dock Assault ships. However, the building of amphibious capability is certainly a sign of assertiveness by the PLA. Despite this, a military offensive against Taiwan remains a distant reality.

China's current assertiveness can be attributed to its present military capability to engage targets by conventional cruise missiles against all littoral regions of the world. This is achievable by the six Type-093 B Shang class nuclear submarines which currently carry 24 VLS CJ-10 cruise missiles with a range of about 2000 km. China is currently developing Type 095 and Type 097 submarines which would have greater capabilities.[23] The Type-093 has moved around Sri Lanka in March 2014. Missiles from these submarines will be targetable by the PLA's constellation of radar and electro-optical surveillance satellites. They would be guided by PLA's Beidou navigation satellite system with links to communication satellites. These missiles with conventional explosives would enable the Chinese leadership to play a decisive role in conflicts across the globe. China today has the capability to militarily assert itself in any conflict with this nuclear submarine—cruise missile combination.

China frequently professes that it does not advocate an arms race in space and would like to ban weapons in this domain. However, the fact is that the PLA has invested considerably in strategic thought and specific technologies needed for wresting eventual control of outer space. It is pertinent to note that the January 2007 ASAT missile demonstration constituted a significant Chinese space development. Possibly, China is seeking superiority in space to dictate the outcome of future conflicts on earth and outer space. This effort will involve the development of specific space combat systems as well as an extensive manned space programme to serve political, scientific and military goals. The space programme of China is controlled by the PLA Specifically, the General Armaments Department (GAD) under the Central Military Commission, develops requirements and controls the entire Space programme. The 2006 White Paper issued by China states that "China considers the development of its space industry as a strategic way to enhance its economic, scientific-technological and national defence strength, as well as a cohesive force for the unity of the Chinese people in order to rejuvenate China."

Further, there are indications that China is preparing to wage a war in outer space. In his book, Space Warfare, Colonel Li Daguang describes potential

PLA operational goals as, "Destroy or temporarily incapacitate all enemy satellites above our territory, deploy land-based and space-based ASAT weapons, counter US missile defence systems, maintain our good international image by covert deployment and have our space strike weapons concealed and launched only in time of crisis.[24]

On July 25, 2014, the US State Department accused China of conducting another ASAT test. The statement read that "The United States has concluded that on 23 July 2014, the People's Republic of China conducted a non-destructive test of a missile designed to destroy satellites. A previous destructive test of the system in 2007 created thousands of pieces of debris which continue to present an ongoing danger to space systems of all stations including China. We call on China to refrain from destabilising actions such as the continued development and testing of destructive anti-satellite systems-that threaten the long term security and sustainability of the outer space environment on which all nations depend. The US continuously looks to ensure its space systems are safe and resilient against emerging space threats." China's Xinhua news agency said that it conducted a successful land-based missile intercept test on July 23, 2014 that achieved its preset goal. The test clearly indicates Chin's importance of ASAT weaponry.[25]

It is probable that China may be researching the feasibility of using unmanned space platforms for both space and earth attack combat missions. Chinese aerospace literature indicates that the PLA may be developing a space-based ground attack system. It implies having a satellite that can attack weapons on earth. The literature describes the use of a war capsule which delivers the weapon through the atmosphere to its target. The greatest advantage of a space-based ground attack weapon system is its high speed and short re-entry time. This makes interception of such a weapon extremely difficult.[26] China has disclosed no information about possible plans for such a platform. However, it is possible to use a space station-like vessel for such purpose. China launched its first space laboratory The Tiangong 1 Space laboratory on September 29, 2011. Tiangong 1 was visited by a series of Shenzhou spacecraft, the last being the manned Shenzhou 10 which docked in June 2013. The Tiangong 2 space station was launched in September 2016 and the Chinese space station which will be based on the International Space Station and is likely to be launched by 2020. There are also Chinese efforts to make a space shuttle or a smaller space plane that could serve a civil or military purpose. Overall, the Chinese are preparing to use outer space for military applications.

Construction of Dams

It has been stated that the next World War will be over water. Tibet is the "water tower" of Asia and rivers originating in Tibet flow into various regions in Asia. They are a lifeline to almost 50 per cent of the world's population residing in South and South East Asia. Further, the Himalayas constitute the largest reservoir of snow and ice in the world outside the polar regions with about 1500 glaciers that drain water into the Himalayan Karakoram river system. China today faces an acute water scarcity due to its huge population, increased industrial development and water-intensive agriculture practices. China does not want its aspirations diluted by a major water crisis. Water and energy security form an important aspect of Chinese architecture. There are three rivers that affect India with regard to Tibet. These are the Brahmaputra, Sutlej and the Indus. It is pertinent to note that these rivers flow out of India into the neighbouring countries.

The Brahmaputra is a major river basin for India and Bangladesh. Since it flows through harsh mountainous terrain, its direct use for the Tibet Autonomous Region may be limited. However, China's plan of creating a South-North linkage of rivers has received attention to the river. As far back as July 2003, a report in the People's Daily gave out that China was conducting a feasibility study for major hydropower projects on the Yarlung Tsangpo. It is understood that there are proposals to construct 28 dams on the river out of which three are under construction. Before entering India, the river passes Pi in Tibet and suddenly turns towards the North and North East and cuts through a succession of great narrow gorges between the mountains Gyala Periand Namjabarwa in a series of rapids and cascades. The river then turns south and south-west and flows through a deep gorge across the eastern extremity of the Himalayas with canyon walls that extend upward of 16500 feet and more on each side. This is the Great Bend where China has plans to build the world's biggest hydropower project of 40,000 megawatts capacity and also divert water from here to North China, though China is currently denying any such plans.[27] The implications of undertaking these measures would have repercussions on India and Bangladesh.

The Sutlej River is the longest of the five rivers that flow through the historic crossroads region of Punjab in Northern India and Pakistan. The source of the river is Lake Rakshastal in Tibet. From there, it flows to the Shipkila Pass in Himachal Pradesh. The Sutlej traverses a distance of 260 km in Tibet. China has constructed one hydroelectric project on the river. The Indus River which commences at Mansarovar in Tibet has reportedly a dam under construction by the Chinese. The dam is to be used for generating hydroelectricity which would enable augmenting China's energy requirements. It is pertinent to note that Tibet is a repository for fresh water in Asia. Apart from these three rivers which flow from Tibet into India, the Mekong flows into Myanmar, Thailand, Laos and Cambodia, and onwards to Vietnam where it enters the South China Sea. Further, the River Salween enters Myanmar and the River Yangtse, which commences from Tibet and has a course of 6300 km, before entering the East China Sea in Shanghai.

Figure 5.2: Dams Planned By China On Brahmaputra[28]

It is interesting to observe that Asia's water resources are largely transnational, making inter-country cooperation essential. The only treaties in Asia with specific sharing formulas on cross-border river flows are the ones between India and its two downstream neighbours Pakistan and Bangladesh. The Indus Waters treaty remains the world's most generous water sharing agreement, under which India agreed to keep only 19.48 per cent of the water share. On the contrary China stands out for not having a single water sharing agreement or cooperation treaty with any co-riparian state. Its refusal to accede to the Mekong Agreement of 1995 has affected the development of a genuine basin community. By building mega dams and reservoirs in its borderlands China is working to unilaterally re-engineer the flows of major rivers that are the livelihood of the lower Riparian states. China has bilateral agreements on research initiatives, flood control projects, hydro-power development, fishing, navigation, hydrological work and sharing of hydrological data. These are by no account water sharing agreements. Thus it is deduced that China does not practice the concept of water sharing with its co-Riparian states. China asserts a general principle that standing and flowing waters are subject to the full sovereignty of the state where they are located. It thus claims indisputable sovereignty over the waters on its side of the international boundary, including the right to divert as much shared water for its legitimate needs. China has rejected the 1997 UN Water Course Convention; placed on record its absolute sovereignty over the waters within its borders. Accordingly, water has become a contentious issue between China and the Riparian states. The PLA being under the Communist Party has played its role in the construction of dams in China.

Former Indian Prime Minister Manmohan Singh personally proposed to Chinese President Xi Jinping and Premier Li Keqiang in separate meetings in 2013, that the two countries enter into a water treaty or establish an inter-governmental institution to define mutual rights and responsibilities on shared rivers. Both Xi and Li, however, spurned the proposal. China's rush to build more dams would further embitter relations between China and the lower Riparian countries. Getting China on board is critical for water peace in Asia.[29]

The aspect of security as it pertains to Asia has undergone tremendous change in the post-Cold War era. In the Asia-Pacific, the US had worked out alliances with Japan, South Korea, Australia and New Zealand, and strategic partnerships with The Philippines and Thailand. Further, there were understandings with Taiwan and Singapore. These strategic measures were primarily against the erstwhile Soviet Union and North Korea. The end of the Cold War has witnessed the phenomenal rise of China. It has also witnessed the US getting involved in resolving conflicts in Iraq, Kosovo, Afghanistan and the Middle East. China has with its rising power turned assertive in all spheres. Managing the rise of China successfully is the most important fundamental challenge confronting the international community in the 21st century. This process is significant not only because it promises the internal transformation of one of the world's oldest civilisations, but also because if concluded successfully, it could result in a dramatic power transition within the international system.[30]

As stated above, the modernisation of the Chinese armed forces has resulted in China becoming more assertive with regard to its continental and maritime claims. Deng Xiao Ping's doctrine of keeping a low profile and building strength seems to have been slowly discarded with the increasing signs of assertiveness visible in the last five years. The latest sign of assertiveness in the maritime domain is the Chinese Belt and Road Initiative which includes the Maritime Silk Road. The proposal made by President Xi Jinping in October 2013 envisages China's desire to establish a foothold in the Indian Ocean by creating infrastructure which would assist it commercially and strategically in an indirect manner. The opaque nature of the project has raised serious doubts about its strategic intentions.[31]

The modernisation of the Chinese armed forces has led to its assertiveness which challenges the existing balance of power in Asia. Robert D Blackwill, a former US Ambassador to India, in an address made to the China Foundation for International and Strategic Studies in Beijing on December 11, 2014, on the "Grand Strategy of the US and China", quoted Henry Kissinger as stating, "In the end, peace can be achieved only by hegemony or Balance of Power." He further amplified that due to the profound differences in history, ideology, strategic culture and domestic policies, the US and China have diametrically opposed and mutually incompatible perceptions regarding the balance of power in Asia. In short, both countries have conflicting grand strategies. While the US is undertaking rebalancing, China has conceptualized the Belt & Road Initiative and the Maritime Silk Route. Militarily, China has conceptualised the Anti-Access/Area Denial (A2 /AD) strategy and the US has countered it with the Air Sea Battle in which preemptive actions are taken to thwart the Chinese launch of a missile system. Overall, the situation is grim with Chinese assertiveness.[32]

The global implication of Chinese assertiveness is that it could possibly lead to military confrontation on land, sea, air, cyber and may be outer space.

The answer lies in confronting the military presence to ensure that China is dissuaded from exacerbating a situation either on Taiwan, the Sino-Indian border, the South China Sea or the East China Sea. This would cater for extreme contingencies. However, there is a need for an inclusive security architecture that can deal with issues in the Asia-Pacific, or what is currently being referred to as the Indo-Pacific region. Possibly the best answer is the evolution of the East Asia Summit of 18 countries taking a turn towards security issues. This organisation has evolved from ASEAN and would be in a position to engage all players providing architecture for security discussions. As progress is made it could include military engagements. Similarly, with the UN Security Council losing its relevance, the G-20 has become a new area for security dialogues. In the recent G-20 Summit, held at Brisbane in mid-November, 2014, US President Barrack Obama placed the security of Asia and climate change at the top of agenda. This is a welcome development as both the East Asia Summit and the G-20 are multilateral engagements. Military preparedness along with engagement through inclusive security architecture would enable us to resolve challenges posed by China's assertiveness.[33] With Donald Trump taking over as the President of the United States, issues are practically in the same direction except for those pertaining to trade.

Deductions

- China has been an assertive nation, from its creation and never believed in pacifism. Currently, its White Papers profess peace, but its actions are not in consonance with its pronouncements.
- The core interest of China is the survival of the current authoritarian system which could be threatened by domestic forces in combination with covert foreign forces. China also looks to the issues pertaining to unification of Taiwan, disputes in the East China Sea and South China Sea as also Tibet.
- Current President Xi Jinping is eloquent about the Chinese dream which primarily focuses on Strength and Wealth. He is a strong leader who is not prepared to compromise on territorial claims. Further, he has given full support to Pakistan in stabilising the Port of Gwadar and building the Pakistan-China Economic Corridor. Gwadar thereby

becomes an outpost of the Chinese merchant and military navies. This poses a direct threat to India's strategic interests.

• In the year 2014, China undertook incursions along the Sino-Indian border, established an ADIZ over the East China Sea and moved a mobile oil rig with escorts to the South China Sea, resulting in a standoff with Vietnam in May 2014. Good sense prevailed otherwise it could have led to violent naval clashes which would have been difficult to control. A similar situation was created in Doklam on the Sino-Indian-Bhutan border but could be resolved amicably after a 73 day standoff.

• China has developed its capabilities in all five domains of warfare which pertain to land, sea, air, cyber and outer space. China has been focusing on its outer space programme and has successfully demonstrated an ASAT missile in 2007, and is on the way to developing secretively weapons for use from outer space. Further, it is reported that China has been demonstrating its cyber capabilities against the US, Japan and India. Writings by Chinese PLA officers speak of wars to settle territorial disputes. Further, China has all along believed in asymmetric warfare which would be effectively used in all five dimensions to assert over its adversaries.

• In terms of strategy, China has developed the Anti-Access, Area Denial (AAAD) strategy to be used to prevent aircraft CBGs from reaching the battle space should there be an offensive on Taiwan. This is being achieved by the usage of the DF-21 D Ballistic Missile, which is capable of engaging an aircraft carrier.

• China's assertiveness can be clearly seen in its unwillingness to follow global conventions on the proliferation of missiles and nuclear weapons. China has given extensive assistance to Pakistan and North Korea to develop its nuclear weapons programme. Further, China has also assisted Iran to a lesser extent in developing its nuclear programme.

• China is currently building three dams on the Brahmaputra River in Tibet. It is also planning to divert the river at the Great Bend which would seriously impact the flow of water into Assam and Bangladesh. Despite the issue being raised at the highest level, China steadily continues to move ahead with its construction. Similar projects are being undertaken at a smaller scale on the River Sutlej.

Overall, China has become assertive and poses a military threat to countries in the East China Sea, South China Sea and the Indo-Tibetan border. China has also proposed the Maritime Silk Route which will possibly witness Pakistan, Sri Lanka, Bangladesh and Myanmar joining it, thereby leading to Chinese ships berthing next to India, which poses an automatic threat to our country. India has to be prepared for a continental and maritime threat from China.

Assessment

China has become assertive and poses a military threat to Taiwan, territories located on the East China Sea and South China Sea and Tibet. It has to counter the US in Taiwan, East China Sea and maybe in the South China Sea. In other areas, India remains the main contender. Viewing its modernisation process and its leadership potential it would be difficult to achieve its objectives as the US and India are transforming their armed forces.

NOTES

1. Chase Kenneth Warren, "Firearms a Global History", Cambridge University Press, ISBN 0521822742, 2003, pp. 32,33 and 59.
2. Crosby Alfred, "Throwing Fire Projectiles technology through History", Cambridge University Press, ISBN 0-521-79158-8, 2002, pp. 100-103.
3. Jia Qingguo, "Learning to Live with the Hegemon; Evolution of China's policy towards the US since the end of Cold War", Journal of Contemporary China, Volume 14 number 44, August 2005.
4. "China, yesterday urged the United States to cancel a massive arms deal to Taiwan", China Daily, 08 January 2010.
5. Nozoma Hayashi, "China's Security Commission targets Western values and other Conventional threats", http://ajw.asahi.com/article/asia/china/AJ 201402120067.
6. Brian Spiegle and Vu Trong Kanh, "China moves oil rig from contested waters", The Wall Street Journal, 16 July 2014.
7. Saibal Dasgupta and Rajat Pandit, "Xi Jinping tells PLA to be ready to win the regional war", Times of India, 23 September 2014.
8. "Interview with Lieutenant General Liu Yazhou of the Air Force of the PLA", Eurasian Review of Geopolitics, January 2005.
9. Michael Pillsbury, "China Debates the Future Security Environment", National Defence University Press, Washington, D.C. 2000.
10. "Xinhua," 30 July 2007.
11. "China Military Online", accessed through Security-Risks.Com, 15 October 2014.
12. Kevin Mc McCauley, "PLA Joint Operations and Military Reform", China Brief, Volume 14, Issue: 7, 09 April 2014.
13. Ashley, J.Tellis, "China's Military Space Strategy", Survival, 2007, p.43.

14. Taiwan Publication, "Mainland China has already deployed, Anti Satellite Laser Artillery", http://www.takungpao.com/news/09/04/26/junshi03-1072048htm, 26 April 2009.
15. Wang Zaigang, "The Nemesis of Super Aircraft Carrier Battle Groups", Naval and Merchant Ships, 05 January 2005, pp.24-27.
16. Richard D Fisher Jr, "China's Military Modernisation", Pentagon Press, New Delhi, 2008, p.175.
17. Cheng Kuaile and Zhang Ping, "Precision Oriented Logistics", Objectives of the logistics revolution in the 21st century by the 21st century by Zhonggo Junshi Keuxe, 20 November 1999, translated on 04 February 2000.
18. Major General S B Asthana, "Transformation of PLA Logistics System: An Analysis", USI, Volume CXLI, Number 586, October-December 2011.
19. "Global Security, Y-20/Y-XX program, History", 04 April 2014.
20. Chang Felix K, "Making Waves: Debates Behind China's First Aircraft Carrier", Foreign Policy Research Institute, October 2012, p.6.
21. Bitzinger Richard A and Mitchell Paul, "Soviet Aircraft Carrier Varyag, Shape of things to come", Raja Ratnam School of International Studies, 06 May 2011 and Chanakaiyee, Exposure of Aircraft Carrier by Liaoning, tianamenstremendousachievements.wordpress.com posted 28 August 2014.
22. "Type 081 Landing Helicopter Dock", Asian Defence, www.asiandefencenews.com/2014/09/is-chines-navy-working-on-081.html, 16 April 2014.
23. "China in a frenzy to build nuclear attack submarines", threat to US security, a consortium of defence analysts at cofda.wordpress.com Posted on 05 July 2014.
24. Books examining the Military requirements of Space Power, Bao Zhangxing, "The Initial Design For Creation of a Space Force", NDU Press, Beijing 1988; Michael Pillsbury, "An Assessment of China's Anti Satellite and Space Warfare Programme, policies and doctrines", Report submitted to the United States-China Economic and Review Commission, 19 January 2004 and Christopher Stone, "Chinese intentions and American preparedness", Space Review, http://www.thespacereview.com/article/930/1, 13 August 2007.
25. Maria S Smith, "US accuses China of conducting another ASAT test", spacepolicyonline.com, 25 July 2014.
26. Yuan Guoxiong, Bai Tao and Ren Zhang, "A Hybrid Re-entry Guidance method for space-based Ground Attack Weapon System", Zhanshu Daodan, Kongzhi Zishu, 01 September 2005, Open Source Centre, CPP2006014424006 and n.50, p.205.
27. Parag Jyoti Saikia, "Brahmaputra-the Beautiful River on the Battle Ground", South Asia network on dams, rivers and people, sandrp.wordpress.com. Posted on 17 July 2013.
28. Times News Network, "Dams on The Brahmaputra", *The Economic Times*, 05 October 2016.
29. Brahma Chellany, "China, Asia's Water Hegemon", Live Mint, 16 September 2014.
30. Michael D Swaine and Ashley J Tellis, "Interpreting China's Grand Strategy Past Present and Future", RAND, Santa Monica, California, USA, 2000, p.1.
31. Abhijit Singh, "China's Maritime Silk Route, Implications for India", IDSA Comment, New Delhi, 16 July 2014.
32. Ambassador Robert D Blackwill, "US-China Diplomacy and Grand Strategy", as prepared for delivering to China Foundation for International and Strategic Studies. 11 December 2014.
33. Renee Lewis, "Obama pushes Asian Security, climate action at G-20 summit in Brisbane", America.aljazeera.com, 15 November 2014.

CHAPTER 6

Implications for India

Introduction

Modernisation of the Chinese armed forces has resulted in China becoming more assertive in its international relations. As far as India is concerned, she has a boundary dispute with China which often leads to transgressions by both countries. India has also firmly pointed out its dislike of China assisting Pakistan in its nuclear programme. The PLA Navy has started making forays into the Indian Ocean which is of concern to India. It is pertinent to note that nuclear-powered submarines of the Song Class have been moving close to Sri Lanka and this has been noted by India as these submarines carry missiles which can engage targets anywhere in India. China has also helped terrorists in Pakistan like Azhar Masood remains free from being tried for terror crimes. China is preventing India from becoming a member of the Nuclear Supply Group.

In the last 69 years, on different occasions, China has conveyed, "historical losses" of territories and these claims are made through its maps and atlases. After the occupation of Tibet, Mao Zedong described Tibet as China's palm with Nepal, Sikkim, Bhutan, Arunachal and Ladakh as its five fingers. A few maps had even claimed that the entire Assam and even the Andamans were historically a part of China. China does not easily settle its territorial and maritime claims. The problem is that no one is aware as to which Chinese era is its territorial benchmark. China recognises the McMahon Line as its boundary with Myanmar but not with India. It is indeed perplexing that till date China has not revealed its perception of the Line of Actual Control (LAC) which could reduce local tension when troops from either side carry out patrolling. Further, it would enable implementation as envisaged in Article 3 of the Agreement on Confidence Building Measures in the military field along the LAC.

Chinese pride and nationalism have also been on the rise. This is evident from its participation in sports, infrastructural development, technological innovation and competing with the best participants in the world. It is believed that such strategic behaviour is conditioned by a strong sense of victimisation and vulnerability arising from past memories of colonialism and principal focus being on sovereignty. There is a strong desire to regain status and influence. Henry Kissinger in his latest book, "On China", states that China's strategy generally exhibits three characteristics: meticulous analysis of long term trends, careful study of tactical options and detached exploration of operational decisions. He described the Chinese style of dealing with strategic decisions as thorough analysis, careful preparation and attention to psychological and political factors as also rapid conclusion.

China's rising global power status can take two possible directions:

- Would act more responsibly in international affairs, go in for more equitable distribution of resources, and contribute to the stability of weaker states that do not have the capacity of legitimate security, thus leading to greater global stability
- Alternately, its intense nationalist sentiments would cause its recent assertive stance to harden, resulting in clashes between existing and emerging powers.[1]

Considering China's issues with India, it is essential to analyse our proposed national security strategy and thereafter analyse the security aspects.

Analysis of the Proposed National Security Strategy

Analysing the Constitution of India, India's national security interests originate from preserving core values and attaining national vision. These could be classified as Vital and Major Interests. Vital interests are as stated below:

- Security of sovereign territory;
- Access to a resource in the Exclusive Economic Zone (EEZ) and energy;
- Internal stability, peace and security;
- Elimination of terrorism/violence by religious/political extremism;
- Free flow of commerce;
- Stable financial systems, international monetary order, the pursuit of science and technology.

Major interests are as under:

- Removal of poverty safeguarding of fundamental rights, providing access to resources and opportunities to all;
- Peace and stability in the neighbourhood as also the Indian Ocean Region;
- Reforming international institutions;
- Orderly and non-discriminatory movement of people across nations;
- Elimination of fugitives from justice;
- Unencumbered access to global commons.

The erstwhile government tried to craft a national security strategy document by a paper Non-Alignment 2.0. This is not an official document and there is an urgent need for formulation of a national security strategy. The paper did not take the views of Service Headquarters. It is pertinent to note the following:

- By 2030, we are heading for a bipolar world with the US and China as the new superpowers.
- India in this bipolar world order appears to be a peripheral player that must safeguard by being non-aligned between China and the United States. In short, India must maintain her strategic autonomy.
- China surrounds our country geographically, has attacked us once in 1962 and is currently engaged in building Pakistan as a local nuclear and conventional military counterweight to India. China tacitly enables Pakistan to wage unrestricted asymmetric warfare against India. It seeks to incite all our SAARC neighbours to adopt assertive stances towards our country and seek to contain India by its "String of Pearls" strategy which has been modified by President Xi Jinping to One Belt One Road in which ports and infrastructure will be built in the Indian Ocean region.
- India has to be prepared for a worst case scenario of facing a two-front conflict involving China and Pakistan. It is essential that India balances Chinese hegemony with an intense strategic relationship with the United States, Japan, Vietnam, Indonesia, The Philippines, Australia and South Korea.
- India's comprehensive national power must dissuade China and deter Pakistan from undertaking a military adventure.

The national security strategy must include non-traditional threats related to water, energy, food and pandemic diseases. There is a need to formulate the national security strategy at the earliest to enable lucid strategic thought and action.[2] Steps have been taken to form a defence policy committee to expedite the issue.

Implications

China's military modernisation, capacity building, infrastructure development in Tibet and forays into the Indian Ocean pose serious challenges to India's security. China's growing footprint in South Asia and attempts to bring peripheral states into its circle of influence only add to these concerns. There is a duality in approaches to dealing with these challenges. While broader political discourse underscores cooperation and downplays competition, there is a growing realisation that India needs to develop credible hard power as a dissuasive strategy against China. India's strategic dilemma lies in shaping its political response to external balancing. Although there is an understanding of strategic convergence between India and the US, there is little consensus on how to shape this relationship to further India's strategic interests. New Delhi continues to face a policy dilemma whether to be a regional balancer, a swing state, or a strategic hedge.

In his book, Samudra Manthan, Professor C Raja Mohan, Director Institute of South Asian Studies, National University of Singapore, deals with the Sino-Indian rivalry in the Indo-Pacific region. The author feels that Sino-Indian ties will shape the 21st century like few other themes over the coming decades. In fact, the triangular relationship between the United States, China and India will be as important as US-Soviet Union relations during the Cold War. The modernisation of the Chinese and the Indian Navies will extend the security dilemma between the two countries. It will express itself in both the Indian and the Pacific Oceans. By 2030, both navies could be involved in a conflict. The book clearly articulates Chinese assertiveness in the Indian Ocean and India's response in the region. The Indian Navy is not described as making forays in the Pacific Ocean. Accordingly, the military modernisation of the Chinese Navy would witness forays by China in the Indian Ocean. The Maritime Silk Route would enable China to build ports and infrastructure in the Indian Ocean which would facilitate Chinese warships to make use of the same for logistics support, indirectly causing security concerns for India.

There are still many gaps about Chinese aspirations in the future. A major component of China's grand strategy is to preserve and enhance its political supremacy as also its influence in Asia without provoking the emergence of a countervailing coalition of states.[3] India's objective is to build a strong economic base that will be capable of supporting its aspirations as a regional power with the same primacy as China in Asia. Burdened by the baggage of history and plagued as it still is by the Middle Kingdom syndrome, China has always had immense difficulty in accommodating India's aspirations as the second Asian power. Despite improving trade relations with India, with the balance of trade in China's favour, China is engaged in a policy aimed at the strategic encirclement of India with a view to stunting its overall growth to prevent it from mounting a challenge to China's hegemony in Asia. The salient ingredients of this strategy are as stated below:

- China seeks to contain India through a nuclear weapons-cum-missile nexus and an extremely strong strategic partnership based on extensive military cooperation with its all-weather ally and friend Pakistan, whose territorial integrity it has guaranteed. It has built the strategic Karakoram Highway linking Xinjiang with Pakistan through the disputed territory of Jammu and Kashmir and now plans to build a railway line as well. It has built a major seaport with the potential for establishing a naval base at Gwadar on the Makran coast.
- China is also engaged in serious attempts to make inroads into India's neighbourhood through Nepal, Bangladesh, Myanmar and Sri Lanka. China offers military aid, military training and subsidised arms to these countries, makes strategic infrastructure investments in them such as the development of ports and absorbs a limited quantity of uneconomical imports from them.
- This is unlikely to change in the near future. China's strategy in Southern Asia is to create alternate incentive structures in India's neighbourhood to prevent the pacification and consolidation of the region.[4]
- While this view is held by members of the Indian strategic community, many perceptive analysts in the West also share it. Quoting a variety of sources, Edward Timperlake and William C. Triplet II have carefully documented how China is engaged in surrounding India and arming India's adversary.[5]

The implication is that China's growing power and influence in Asia poses a long term strategic challenge to India. Competition for markets and political influence between these two Asian giants could become unhealthy in the future. In view of the unresolved territorial and boundary disputes between the two countries and aggressive military posturing on China's part at the tactical level, possibilities of a conflict cannot be ruled out.[6]

While the focus of China's military modernisation in the immediate short term appears to be preparing for a potential conflict in the Taiwan Strait, an analysis of military procurements indicates that China is preparing for settling issues beyond the Taiwan Strait. China has a disputed border with India and of late its transgressions have increased. The Chinese economy is slowing down and the increase in labour prices is increasing the price of products, thereby impacting exports. Further, in the current trade war between US and China tariffs have been imposed by President Trump which makes Chinese goods costlier. This would impact exports. China is an export-driven economy and reduction in exports would have an adverse effect on the rate of growth. This would affect domestic sensitivity which could be diverted by possibly undertaking operations to resolve the border with India.

It is evident that factors which could lead to hostilities exist. This could manifest itself in a variety of ways. A possible way is enumerated. Prior to the onset of hostilities, the strategic stage of the conflict would be set through the three warfare's—psychological, public opinion and legal. This may well be a year or more prior to the conflict. This would be followed by numerous meetings to resolve issues keeping Chinese views into consideration. A possible conflict could work out as enumerated below:

- Cyber-attacks to hit at Indian financial and economic institutions;
- Exploiting the full range of space warfare capabilities to achieve space dominance;;
- Concentrated Short Range Ballistic Missiles (SRBM) attacks on key command and communication nodes;
- Integrated Network Electronic Warfare. This concept integrates Electronic Warfare, Computer Network Operations to undertake kinetic strikes against key Command, Control, Communication and Computer Nodes.

The Chinese would seek conflict termination at each stage of the escalatory ladder. The buildup of troops from the Western Theatre Command into the Tibetan Autonomous Region would continue simultaneously. Thereafter, we could expect a ground offensive which could be coupled with naval action to ensure Chinese shipping is not affected in the Indian Ocean Region by the Indian Navy.[7]

India has to be prepared to conduct successful operations which would require blunting the Chinese offensive at each stage. We would require a very high capability in Network Centric Warfare (NCW), Electronic Warfare (EW) and Space Warfare. It is commendable that India is working positively in these fields. It is essential that the Indian Air Force (IAF) has dominance over the Tibetan Plateau if successful operations have to be undertaken by India. To militate against an attack by missiles we need a credible a Ballistic Missile Defence (BMD) as also a modernised army which can thwart the Chinese offensive. The Indian Navy should be able to outwit the PLA Navy in the Indian Ocean. Overall, the Indian strategy must raise its level of preparations from dissuasion to deterrence. The present government has worked fervently in this direction.

Analysis

China's military modernisation poses a serious challenge to Indian security along the disputed border and the Indian Ocean. By 2030, China's assertiveness could lead to situations of conflict with India. Further, China is engaged in surrounding India and arming Pakistan to asymmetrically conduct a low-intensity conflict against India. While the focus of China may be on Taiwan, the disputed border with India is witnessing sporadic transgressions. The slowing down of the Chinese economy could compel the PLA to launch an offensive against India which would be a combination of cyber, ASAT weapons, missile attacks, Integrated Network Electronic Warfare and multiple intrusions. India must leave no stone unturned to modernise its military capability to meet this eventuality.

Assessment

China has accelerated its modernisation process and its forces pose a continental and maritime threat to India. India on her part is aware of the same and closely observing China at the border and the Indian Ocean region. The Chinese, in case of a conflict, would meet stiff resistance and would not be in a position to achieve their objectives despite a collusive threat from China and Pakistan. Notwithstanding the same, India must accelerate the modernisation of its armed forces.

NOTES

1. General V P Malik, "Foreword China's Defence Policy, Indian Perspective, CLAWS, *KW Publishers Private Limited*, New Delhi, 2011, pp. ix–xi.
2. Major General G D Bakshi, "India's National Security Crisis, Chapter-6, Non-Alignment 2.0, An Analysis of proposed national security," *Bloomsbury Publishing India Private Limited*, New Delhi, 2014, pp.118-120.
3. Alec Liebman, "China's Asia policy, strategy and tactics; paper focuses on, The PLA in the Asia Pacific region, implications for the evolving Regional security Order, 08-10 December 2006.
4. Brigadier Gurmeet Kanwal, "Chinese Defence Policy, Indian Perspective, Centre for Land Warfare Studies, *KW Publishers Private Limited*, New Delhi, 2011.
5. Edward Timperlake and William C Triplet, "Red Dragon Rising, Communist China's Military threat to America," *Regency Publishing Inc*, Washington D. C. 1999, p. 21.
6. Brig Gurmeet Kanwal, "Chinese Defence Policy Indian Perspective, Centre for Land Warfare Studies, *KW Publishers Private Limited*, New Delhi, 2011, p. 21.
7. Ibid, pp. 151-154.

*

CHAPTER 7

Optimisation of Assets in a Conflict

Introduction

The post-Second World War international system has evolved from a sharply bipolar world into a unipolar world order dominated by the United States and its Western allies. As on date, there are 56 alliance partners of the US. As the power of the US has waned due to imperial overstretch, it has now become an asymmetric unipolar world order, where US is still the dominant military, economic and technological power but is being increasingly constrained by rising regional powers, which can check its influence in their own backyards and raise the costs of US military interventions. The military interventions in Iraq and Afghanistan have clearly demonstrated the inability of Western Powers to commit boots on the ground for more than 15 years. By and large, most US interventions in the future will entail no committal of ground troops but mostly employment of firepower in terms of cruise missiles stealth bomber and fighter attacks with drones firing precision guided munitions. Given the cost of fighting militants, the United States is not in a position to enforce a prolonged occupation of any country.

The world is witnessing the ascendancy of China which is gradually extending its sphere of influence. Further, the global centre of gravity has shifted decisively from Europe to Asia. Today Asia has seven out of the world's 10 major economies and a sizeable part of the nuclear weapon powers.

The rise of Asia has also witnessed the rise of tensions. The modernization of the Chinese armed forces and its politico-military friendship with Pakistan could lead to the following:

- **India-Pakistan War** (with or without Chinese involvement). With the rise of tensions over Pakistan sponsored terrorism, there are increasing possibilities of a major terrorist strike, which escalates into an Indian military response and results in a limited conventional war against a nuclear overhang between India and Pakistan. This conflict could remain confined to Jammu and Kashmir or spill over across the International Border in Punjab and Rajasthan. The war could possibly escalate and there is likelihood of India attempting a blockade of ports in Pakistan. The two ports of Gwadar and Karachi are possibly going to be blocked. Further, air and missile strikes will be undertaken against refineries and other economic targets. It would indeed be a challenge to ensure this limited war to be below the nuclear threshold and this would place major emphasis on escalation control dynamics. It would obviously affect the Indian economy as also possibly cripple the Pak economy. It is pertinent to note that threat of Chinese intervention in such a conflict would be possible and India may need overwhelming support of the United States to deter Chinese intervention.

• **Sino-Indian Conflict.** China may not enter a conflict triggered by Pakistan. However, Pakistan is most likely to take advantage of any India-China conflict. The conflict could be based on the border issue coupled with the domestic situation in China which could lead to a diversion of the issue by going into a conflict with India.[1]

Drivers of Conflict

Managing the rise of China with its extensive military modernisation is going to be a difficult issue. It is also clear that India would offer stiff resistance. The drivers of conflict could be as discussed in the following paragraphs.

The Tibetan Issue. Tibet remains a core issue between India and China. India would like China to begin a process of reconciliation and healing in Tibet in its own interest and stable Sino-Indian relations. Beijing has linked Arunachal as a part of Tibet and has been claiming the entire state. Further, China has been building dams on the River Brahmaputra and tampering with the flow at the Great Bend. Further, the choice of the new Dalai Lama is causing consternation in the region. All these issues could exacerbate and result in issues going out of control. Being a sensitive issue, this could result in hostilities.[2]

India–US strategic Partnership. Signaling renewed intensity in ties, India and the US on January 25, 2015 decided to further elevate their long-standing strategic partnership by enhancing cooperation in a raft of crucial areas to include defence, trade and commerce, technology transfer, counter-terrorism and climate change.[3] The joint declaration mentions about freedom of navigation and freedom of flight which refers to the oceans and the skies. In his Republic Day message, the US President has offered to lift the strategic partnership to a higher level. An article that appeared in the Global Times and People's Daily on January 25, 2015 cautioned India not to fall into the trap, which was being laid to pit New Delhi against Beijing. It added that many Western media reports have pointed out that the US regardless of historical complications, is putting more efforts into soliciting India to act as a partner, even an ally, to support Washington's pivot to Asia strategy, which is mainly devised to counter China's rise. In a further elaboration, the daily pointed to the West's ulterior motive to frame the Chinese dragon and the Indian elephant as natural rivals. The West is egging India to be fully prepared for threats by rivals.[4] These issues can cause provocation which could throw things out of control. The Quad which remains a diplomatic partnership between the US, Japan, Australia and India could gradually transform into a military partnership making issues more serious between China and India.

High Profile Posturing in the Indian Ocean Region. Reports emanating from Beijing indicate that China is contemplating setting up military bases overseas to counter American influence and exert pressure on India. This has been interpreted by some sections as a veiled reference to China's interest in securing a permanent military presence in Pakistan. Although it might not be politically feasible for the Pakistan Government to openly allow China to set up a military base, New Delhi fears that Islamabad might allow Beijing use of its military facilities without any public announcement. It is possible to explain the construction of these ports and facilities by China on purely economic and commercial grounds, but regional and global powers like the US, Japan and India inevitably view the sum total of China's diplomatic and military efforts in the Indian Ocean as projecting power vis-a-vis competing rivals. Moreover, most Chinese naval facilities in the Indian Ocean are dual use in nature and no serious strategy can discount their future military use. The notion that China aspires to dominate the Indian Ocean is a bit far-fetched. However, China wishes to play a greater role in the region, to protect and advance its interests, especially Chinese commercial interests, as well as to counter India. Countering India will be a difficult task given the immense geographical advantages that India enjoys in the Indian Ocean. Even the task of protecting the Sea Lines of Communication (SLOC) remains challenging for the PLA Navy as of now. Currently, the steps that China is taking have caused concern. In 2009, a sonar standoff is reported to have taken place between the Indian and Chinese Navies while their ships were proceeding to the Gulf of Aden.[5] In 2014, two incidents of Chinese submarines visiting Sri Lanka were viewed by India with concern. As both navies get stronger such posturing might lead to accidental conflagration which could result in confrontation. It is reported that Chinese nuclear submarines sporadically foray into the Indian Ocean.

The Water Issue. The taming of the Brahmaputra by China could have major implications for India. China certainly wants to utilise Tibetan water resources for its development. It is presumed that one day China may divert waters from the Great Bend of the Yarlung Tsangpo (River Brahmaputra), north of the McMahon Line building another mammoth dam, much bigger than the Three Gorges Dam, which currently is the biggest dam in the world. China has viewed Engineer Guo Kai's 'Shuotian Canal Project' as a perfect model which would save China with Tibet's waters. In addition, this will be another gigantic power plant with an astonishing generating capacity of 20 to 40,000 megawatts. This, if constructed, will be three times bigger than the hydroelectric plant at the Three Gorges Dam. This one plant can fulfill five times the energy requirement of Bangladesh. The taming of this river will require explosives of a very high magnitude. The impact would be profound and impact the people of North East India and Bangladesh. Further, the area being seismically unstable; the construction of the dam would cause severe earthquakes. In addition, there is a proposal to build 28 dams on the Brahmaputra, which would sequester silt that normally gets washed to the flood plains of India and Bangladesh renewing fertility of their agricultural lands. All this is bound to exacerbate tensions and could lead to hostilities.[6]

Collapse of Pakistan. Pakistan is an unstable state with factionalism running against dominant Punjabis by groups from Baluchistan and the North West Frontier Province. There are issues between Sindhis, Punjabis and the Baluchis which could cause friction as also problems with the Shia population of Gilgit-

Baltistan. Further, the ethnic divide has been exacerbated by the Inter-Services Intelligence of Pakistan which has links with numerous terrorist groups operating in Pakistan. Some of the terror groups operate against Afghanistan, some against India and some against Pakistan. The economy is in doldrums and politicians are destabilising the country. The Pakistan armed forces contain few Islamic elements who are in league with these terror groups. All these could result in a collapse of the state and the Chinese would see an India hand in it which could lead to China teaching a lesson to India.

Border Dispute. The border dispute remains unresolved and there are sporadic standoffs between troops deployed on both sides. There have been altercations and it does not take long for a small incident to get blown up to accidents. The current stalemate is dangerous and could lead to hostilities between the two sides. The Indian Prime Minister visited China in May 2015. Despite friendly talks, he has stated that the border issue is like a tooth ache which could easily conflagrate into hostilities.[7] The issue was raised during the informal Wuhan Summit between President Xi Jinping and Prime Minister Modi on April 27-28, 2018. Both sides directed their militaries to earnestly implement various confidence building measures in the border areas.

Likely Strategic Scenarios

Based on the drivers of Conflict Escalatory Dominance, three alternate scenarios could emerge for the South Asian region. These are as elucidated in following paragraphs.

Strategic Brinkmanship. This is the current scenario where leaders of the region have failed to dispel regional mistrust and suspicion. Compelled by the increasing socio-political, economic and security challenges smaller South Asian nations seek support of bigger nations. Both India and China are willing to provide support. China along with Pakistan, is keeping India tied down with sporadic border aggression in the North and routine infiltration attempts as also violations on the Line of Control (LOC) on the West. Owing to the compulsion of domestic politics and lack of timely reforms, the Indian economic growth suffers. The sign posts of this scenario are as under:

- Political and diplomatic posturing like grant of visa and exchange of visits;

- Economic cooperation in terms of export/import and market access;
- Creeping assertiveness including border intrusions and transgressions;
- Strengthening of Sino-Pakistan nexus;
- Repeated attempts to influence states of Nepal, Bangladesh, Bhutan, Sri Lanka, Bangladesh and Maldives;
- Covert support to Indian insurgent groups and Maoists;
- Leveraging water resources;
- Increased cyber espionage and sabotage against Vulnerable Areas/ Vulnerable Points;
- Enhanced activities along the border and strategic highways in the cover of exercises;
- Regular demonstration of disruptive technologies.

The impact will be growing Chinese influence in Indian neighbourhood. India would be threatened with growing asymmetric threats and posturing by the PLA.

India-Centric South Asia. The scenario envisages India stepping up its efforts towards political stability, diplomatic initiatives and undertaking reforms to accelerate economic growth resulting in higher Gross Domestic Product and Comprehensive National Power, which effectively reduces the gap with China. India can take a lead in forging strategic multilateral partnerships with its neighbours, thereby effectively reducing the mistrust and gradually dispersing anti-India feelings. The indications would be as under:

- Greater political cohesiveness and revival of economic growth;
- Rapid military modernisation;
- Building of credible asymmetric deterrence capabilities;
- Creation of bilateral or multilateral strategic partnerships;
- Effective control by security forces on the internal situation;
- Developing special strategic relations with US and other countries of Asia Pacific and East Asia.

The impact would be a pro-India outlook amongst South Asian states and lead to greater regional cooperation. It would also restrict the manoeuvring space of a true regional power in South Asia.

Sino-Centric South Asia. This scenario will occur if India continues to falter on economic growth resulting in slow military modernisation and social development. India lacks initiative and fails to resolve outstanding issues with its neighbours. The Sino-Pakistan nexus will get stronger and China would step in as the balancer for the smaller South Asian nations. The sign posts would be as under:

- China's continued growth in Comprehensive National Power;
- India stumbles in economic growth;
- Slowdown in military modernisation;
- Lack of reforms for other modernisation;
- Absence of Indian political and diplomatic initiatives resulting in istrust in the region;
- Strengthening of the Sino-Pakistan nexus;
- Indo-US relations stagnant;
- Stable Sino-US and US-Pak relations;
- Enhanced Chinese economic and military support to smaller South Asian nations.

The impact would be Chinese supremacy in South Asia. China's supremacy would encourage Pakistan to be more belligerent towards India.

Sino-Indian Condominium. A scenario like this is possible when India continues with its economic growth whereas Chinese growth rate stagnates or reduces owing to internal or sub-regional compulsions. In such a scenario, China may take its initiative to forge cooperation with India. In such an eventuality, India can retain its strategic status in the region without interfering with China's status in East Asia and Asia Pacific. Indicators would be as follows:

- Good growth of Indian economy;
- Fast paced military modernization;
- China falters in economic growth resulting in slowing down of military modernization;
- Growing internal unrest in China;
- Stable Indo-US relations;
- Relative stability in Indo Pak relations and weakening Sino-Pak nexus.

The impact will be a win-win situation for both India and China, resulting in strategic stability for both the countries.

Conflict Escalation Scenarios

The situation between a modernised China and India are extremely complex and characterised by mistrust. The visualised coercive scenarios are as elucidated hereafter.

Coercive Scenario I. China subdues India (Coercive Muscle Flexing). In this scenario sustained the growth of China leads to increase in Comprehensive National Power (CNP) which induces a gravitational pull on the South Asian countries and they pursue politico-economic and security choices which are in synchronisation with China's strategic objectives. Further, China incrementally upgrades its commercial presence in the Indian Ocean Region to a military level by establishing surveillance and communication posts, logistics facilities for the visiting naval vessels, enhancing its deployment in the Gulf of Aden and increasing frequency of port calls and joint military exercises. As a matter of fact, the 'String of Pearls' assumes a military dimension. In this scenario, Pakistan is able to manage a semblance of stability, distances itself from the US and heavily relies on China for its survival and sustenance as a nation state. There is a truce between Jihadi elements and alignment between Taliban, Pakistan and China in Afghanistan where as China remains subtly in touch with non-Pashtun elements. In this scenario, India grapples with Left Wing Extremism (LWE) and Pan India Terrorism. Further borders of India remain tense with China and Pakistan. India's economy does not grow optimally and it is unable to allocate adequate financial resources for its intended transformation from a dissuasive to deterrence capability. This scenario will lead India to strategic coercion and will be ripe for China's strategy of subduing the enemy without fighting. China will emerge as a major Asian power and will tilt the balance of power in South Asia and the Indian Ocean Region (IOR) in her favour.

Conflict Scenario II. India trounces Pakistan; in which China postures. In this scenario, it is envisaged that India is making slow but steady progress and is able to maintain her domination in South Asia despite China's increase in CNP and forays into the South Asian strategic space. India-China relations remain steady and stable. India, however, remains embroiled in the growing threat from Left Wing Extremism (LWE) and simmering insurgencies in the North East. Meanwhile, the Taliban are relentlessly attacking the Afghan

National Security Forces and have achieved limited success. Jihadists with tacit support from Pakistan establishment escalate the proxy war against India. A series of sensational terrorist strikes against soft and sensitive targets provoke India to strike at the terrorist infrastructure inside Pakistan by using Precision Guided Munitions (PGM) artillery strikes. Retaliation from India is declared as an act of war by Pakistan which threatens to use nuclear weapons should India up the ante. Jihadi outfits declare a truce and join Pakistan's military clamouring for an all-out Jihad against India. China cautions India against a full-fledged military action against Pakistan. China renders diplomatic and hardware support to Pakistan. China increases its naval deployment along the Gulf of Aden and the East African coast. There are large scale movements of convoys along the Karakoram highway. Reports indicate an increase in patrolling activities along the Line of Actual Control (LAC) and training of formations in Qinghai and Yunnan. In this scenario, there is a need for a strong punitive deterrence capability against Pakistan while maintaining a deterrence posture against IOR and a dissuasive posture against China.

Conflict Scenario III. India confronts China; Pakistan postures. This scenario takes into account China's intention to provoke India into a military conflict with a view to causing politico military embarrassment to it. The reason for China to exercise military option could range from internal dynamics to a perceived sense of relative superiority or strategic miscalculation or even due to an accidental flare up. Having triggered a local skirmish, China could occupy Indian territory in lightly held areas as per its claim line. They could employ pre-acclimatised troops who are prepositioned. China would then resort to strike important Vulnerable Areas and Vulnerable Positions using Non-Contact Asymmetric capabilities. In the meantime, China could mobilise its War Zone campaign forces for launching offensive cycles against Indian Army. As far as the Indian Ocean region is concerned China would prefer to employ Anti Access and Area Denial capability based on submarines, and ASAT weapons while deploying its flotilla to protect SLOCs. In the event of a major confrontation with China, depending on the internal situation in Pakistan, it could range options from heightening proxy war to heating up the LOC, forward posturing and even grab actions. This scenario assumes that Pakistan will not be in a position to open a second front against India in a classical manner. This scenario, if it is played out, can bring out a strong dissuasive capability against Pakistan while maintaining a strong deterrence posture and Quid Pro Quo capability against China.

Conflict Scenario IV. India confronts China and Pakistan (Collusive Hybrid War). This is a worst-case scenario wherein China and Pakistan weave of a design of collusive hybrid threat over a period of time. It would entail covert support to LWE, fueling insurgencies in North East India, enhancing the proxy war in Jammu and Kashmir and other secessionist movements in the country. Acts of cyber espionage, cyber sabotage and weakening of financial systems in the country could form a part of this strategy. An economically weakened and politically fragile Indian state would lend itself to such machinations. The purported intent of such a strategy would be to internally weaken India to a stage where chancing of the success of external aggression brightens. China and Pakistan could act in tandem to subject India to a spatial squeeze by increasing their naval presence in the Indian Ocean region in the form of joint naval exercises. China could resort to indirect posturing in Tibet by using Tibetan unrest or conducting military exercises. Enhanced Chinese presence in the Northern Area will be another sign post in this area. For a collusive hybrid threat strategy to succeed it is important that Indian formations deployed on the Pakistani border remain pinned down so that China is able to render a decisive blow to India. To that end, it may be assumed that the Pakistan border gets activated first. Pakistan could provoke India by undertaking sensational high terrorist strikes against high profile, high pay off targets and along the LOC. Once conflict with Pakistan is triggered, concurrently China could up the ante by grabbing Indian territory in claimed areas and key point strikes as elucidated in the previous scenario. Pakistan could undertake limited offensive actions in the LOC sector while maintaining a strong defensive posture on the International Boundary. China would employ Anti Access Area Denial and protect SLOCs in the IOR. This is the most difficult scenario for India. It entails balancing the Internal Security Situation, adjusting the Army and Air Force formations between the two fronts as also posturing the Indian Navy correctly in the IOR.

Choices in Terms of Strategy

The scenarios depicted above indicate that the modernisation of PLA would make China more assertive. India would have to be prepared to meet the challenge of a broad spectrum of conflicts ranging from coercive to limited war to a wider conflict against both China and Pakistan. Our military deterrence capability will have to be based on the type, nature, level, scale and the intensity of the conflict. Accordingly, the strategic choices that India can exercise to have a favourable strategic balance in future are as under:

- *Adapt to China driven South Asia*: India will have to accept a China-driven South Asia if its economy falters which will affect Comprehensive National Development. Due to the failing economy, India will not be in a position to diplomatically influence her neighbours. This will increase China's gravitational pull in South Asia and will also strengthen the Sino-Pakistan nexus against India. China will dominate the strategic space of South Asia and India will have to accept it since India will lack the power and resources to maintain its influence in the region. Axiomatically, acceptance of this reality would seriously undermine India's neighbours. In such a scenario India's neighbours will ally with China to maximise their national interest. There is also a possibility of them getting aggressive with India at the behest of China.

- *Bind with the US Counter Balance*: Nations mainly resort to external balancing when they fail to balance an adversary through internal balancing. India too can exercise this option in case it finds it difficult to catch up with China entirely on its own. India can consider a strategic alliance with the US and its allies in the Asia Pacific. She can thereby become the linchpin of the US-Asia pivot strategy. In a way, adopting such a strategy also mitigates the Pakistan factor, especially if the Af Pak region is kept on the boil to tie down Pakistan. In the ultimate cost-benefit analysis, the points which merit critical action are; 'Will China be deterred from such a move and seek rapprochement with India,' 'or will it irk China and its hostility towards India will grow? 'On the other hand, will the US risk its relationship with China, if there is a standoff between India and China? The major drawback of this strategy would be that India would be constrained to compromise her strategic autonomy and would have to accommodate the US interests in the Asia-Pacific. India would be seen as a client of the US which will lead to loss of influence. Indian neighbours will try to possibly balance India-US by allying with China.

- Strategic autonomy with interest-based strategic alignments (Special Partnerships). India has followed the non-alignment policy and it was the founder member of the Non-Aligned Movement. This strategic choice bodes well with Indian foreign policy underpinnings premised on the core belief that India is too big a country to come under the tutelage of any external power. In this option, India makes a determined effort to develop her CNP, attains credible deterrence on her own and also seeks interest based strategic alignments (or special partnerships) with the US, East Asian countries and ASEAN. This would enable India to work towards a multipolar Asia, interlocking India's collaborative security and economic interests with those of the other countries in the region. This is essentially a strategy of necessity and seeking cooperative relations in the Asian structure. This strategy demands sustained economic development, astute and proactive diplomacy and credible deterrence capabilities. This will enhance India's prominent role in South Asia and indicate its capability to manage the region. In such a case the South Asian nations will balance between India and China as also stay neutral in a potential conflict between these countries.

Out of the three choices, it would be prudent to adopt the Strategic Autonomy which enables India to correctly respond to the rise of the PLA in future. It would be prudent to state that India is working towards this strategy.

Analysis

The modernisation of the PLA could lead to a possible Sino-Indian conflict. The drivers could be the Tibetan issue, India's special partnership with the US, posturing in the Indian Ocean, the collapse of Pakistan, water issue and finally the border dispute. While India has to be prepared in all five dimensions for a military conflict she would best maintain strategic autonomy with special partnerships.

It is interesting to note that China released its tenth biennial White Paper in the last week of May 2015. This paper, unlike the preceding paper, focuses on specific aspects of national security. As per the paper, China will follow a strategy of Active Defence. Four critical security domains have been highlighted in the paper. These are the ocean, outer space, cyberspace and nuclear deterrence. China is stated to have a million laptop warriors and their recent cyber-attacks against Taiwan, United States and India indicate its ability to undertake Information Warfare. They are prepared to take the battle into adversary's territory in order to inflict substantial damage and disrupt logistics to gain psychological ascendancy. According to Douglas Paal of the Carnegie Endowment For International Peace, Washington, "China's lips say they have no expansionist ambitions but the body language says, Get Out Of My Way."

With regard to India, China's modernisation will create an Asymmetry in the Comprehensive National Power of the two countries. This automatically puts China in a higher pedestal which could possibly lead to a conflict situation which would be dangerous for India. India has to build itself economically and militarily to deter China from undertaking a misadventure. It is heartening to note that since 2014, India is addressing all these issues and would stand up to any Chinese misadventure.

Assessment

There are possibilities of a conflict between China and India. Chinese Armed Forces are modernising at an accelerated pace. Indian Armed Forces are modernising and have the capacity of stiffly resisting Chinese offensives and it is likely they would be able to take the battle to Chinese territory. India's accelerated modernisation will deter a Chinese offensive. Necessary steps need to be taken to prepare accordingly.

NOTES

1. Major General G D Bakshi, "India's National Security Crisis, Chapter-6 Non-Alignment 2.0. An analysis of proposed national security", Bloomsbury Publishing India Private Limited, New Delhi, 2014, pp. 117-122.
2. Brahma Chellany, "Why Tibet remains the core issue in India China relations", *Forbes magazine*, forbes.com, 27 November 2014.
3. "India-US release declaration of friendship to elevate strategic partnership", *The Times of India*, 25 January 2015.
4. "In Republic Day message, China tells India don't fall into the trap laid by the US", *The Times of India*, 26 January 2015.
5. Harsh.V. Pant, "China's naval expansion in the Indian Ocean and India-China rivalry", *The Asia Pacific Journal: Japan Focus*, www.japanforces.org/-Harsh_V_Pant/3353.
6. The Himalayan Voice, "China and India race for dams on River Brahmaputra; Impacts could be massive and unknown", strategichumanalliance.blogspot.com, 04 December 2014.
7. Press Trust of India, "Eagerly looking forward to China visit", economictimes.indiatimes.com, 13 February 2015.

CHAPTER 8
Epilogue

Issues of Importance

Recently, the Chinese economy is experiencing a low growth rate of GDP of 6.5 per cent against a high of 10 per cent eight years ago. China is straining every sinew to negotiate the trade war and put the economy back on rails. They have technocrats in their political hierarchy and would ensure that measures are taken to reduce the debt and the economy gradually shifts from an export-driven economy to a high consumer economy.

Meanwhile, military modernisation moves at a steady pace. China's PLA would have modernised by about 2030 enhancing its CNP exponentially. China by this time would be capable of launching operations in all five domains land, sea, air, outer space and cyber. Though the quality of equipment and skill would be marginally less than world-class standards, China is reducing its strength of the Land Forces and increasing the strength of the Navy, Air Force, Rocket Force and Strategic Support Force. This would make it more assertive in its claims as also in its conduct in International relations. India is a strategic competitor to China and its preeminence in South Asia is critical to its status as an Asian power and important global player. The challenge of a modernised China needs to be addressed to ensure that India continues to grow as a global player. The next 15 years would be extremely important for India on the domestic front. India must economically grow in consonance with the aspirations of the people to improve its CNP. Economic well-being, access to energy resources, the sufficiency of water and technological advancement are the keys to Comprehensive National Development. India continues to face the rising spectre of LWE, simmering insurgencies, proxy wars and pan India terrorism which includes nuclear terrorism making internal security a formidable challenge. India's volatile neighbourhood further complicates India's national security calculus. The nuclear issue is perplexing in as much as China and Pakistan are concerned. The situation is further exacerbated by the introduction of tactical nuclear weapons. China is not only modernising its Second Artillery (PLA Rocket Force) but remains ambiguous about its No First Use doctrine. The drawdown of the international security forces from Afghanistan is being steadily watched particularly with the introduction of radical Islamic State of Iraq and Syria (ISIS) finding its feet in the Northern portions of the country. Globally, Indo Pacific is witnessing a power shift with ensuing strategic brinkmanship between the US and China.

In this strategic milieu, India has an opportunity to leverage as a strategic swing state and enhance its own image as also its status. Accordingly, it becomes imperative for the government to make a comprehensive strategy to ensure that India successfully develops her CNP through sustained development, astute diplomacy and effective deterrence. Strategic configuration of CNP will enable India to dissuade China from any misadventure and consolidate its preeminence of South Asia. To deal with an assertive China and have a favourable strategic balance in South Asia, India needs internal consolidation, be the anchor of South Asian economic integration, a provider of net security by strong deterrence. To achieve these goals, salient aspects required to achieve Comprehensive National Development and Deterrence are elucidated in succeeding paragraphs. At the outset, it is stated that considerable work is being undertaken to make the armed forces strong to face any eventuality.

CNP

Formulation of Policies. It is common knowledge that India's divisive politics and lack of strategic culture hampers efforts to articulate a realistic National Vision, formulate a National Security Strategy and policy formulation on vital issues of national importance. A concerted effort is needed to reverse this trend by undertaking initiatives to develop political consensus on India's national vision, interests and strategic objectives. The Raksha Mantri must have a Task Force comprising Colonel, Captain and Group Captain with vibrant bureaucrats to undertake this task.

Comprehensive National Development. Fundamental to India's National Security is Comprehensive National Development. Sustained and inclusive economic growth above a mark of 7.5 per cent of Gross Domestic Product (GDP), good governance, enabling skill development in the youth, ensuring probity in public life need to be addressed at the earliest. There is an emergent need to undertake social and economic development.

Social Development. The following measures need to be taken towards social development:

- **Improving Governance**. Our efforts to achieve rapid and inclusive development will come to naught, if the issue of governance deficit is not addressed adequately, both in the manner in which public programmes are implemented and the way, the Government interacts with the ordinary citizen. Corruption is endemic in all spheres causing social decay and repulsing Foreign Direct Investment. The legal system in India is respected for its independence but it suffers from notorious delays in dispensing justice. Fundamental reforms are needed in the system to enable justice to be made affordable and delivered with speed. Administrative and police machinery need to be reformed to restore public faith in the system and facilitate speedy decision making and delivery.

- **Developing Human Resources**. The emphasis on tertiary education to include pockets of excellence like Indian Institute of Technology, Indian Institute of Management has paid us rich dividends. There is a need to focus on primary and secondary education which would lead us to areas of skill development. To ensure a continuous and growing supply of quality manpower we need large investments in public sector institutions of higher learning, combined with fundamental reforms of the curriculum and also better service conditions to attract good faculty. The scope for expanding capacity private sector initiatives in higher learning must also be fully exploited. Unless this is done on an urgent basis we will fail to attain global standards. Further, the industry also requires persons skilled in specific trades and the situation in this area is not comforting. India has lagged behind in the area of vocational training and even today enrolment rates in Industrial Technical Institutes, nursing and computer training schools is minim impetus to vocational training and higher learning is essential to transform youth bulge into Demographic Dividend. Further, all these aspects would make India a knowledge hub for South Asia.

- **Innovation**. Knowledge without innovation is of no value. We must improve our capacity to innovate and this would require an all-pervasive change of attitude towards life and work. Further, it would entail a shift from a culture of drift to a culture of dynamism. India has sent a Mission to Mars but while meeting the Chinese threat we need to develop engines for our ships, aircraft and tanks. Similarly, our Make in India projects must be built gradually with our own designed components and Transfer of Technology should lead to fully developed equipment with Indian components. We must now move to create in India.

- **Agriculture.** The most formidable challenge is in the agriculture sector. The average operational land holdings of a farmer are small with no assured irrigation. Over half of the farm holdings do not get institutional credit and are dependent upon money lenders. Agriculture growth has averaged below three per cent. While a number of corrective steps have been taken, the time has come to make a determined and decisive intervention in agriculture in order to boost production and productivity. Higher agricultural output is critical for ensuring Food Security. The National Commission on farmers has drawn attention to the knowledge deficit, which constrains Agricultural productivity. Further, there is a need to focus on and enlarge our agro-based industry.

Economic Development. To ensure desired economic development the following steps need to be taken:

- **Initiating Second Generation Economic Reforms.** The present government is trying its best to initiate second generation reforms. The problem is in passing bills in the Upper House where it does not possess the requisite majority. The government has passed the Goods and Services Tax bill. Second generation reforms may be seen as the set of measures needed to enable a country to attain in a sustained way, high-quality growth. The Chinese have successfully managed a high growth rate which has enabled them to utilise resources for modernising the PLA.

- **Inclusive Growth Aimed at Decreasing Poverty.** India has to make sure that fruits of its economic development reach every section of the society. Naxalism and insurgency in the North East can be tackled if socio-economic development of these areas is done without delay. Grievances of certain sections of the society (women, Muslims and poor) should be addressed so that they become stakeholders in Indian development. These measures will go a long way in addressing some of the fundamental causes of social unrest and tensions.

- **Increasing manufacturing competitiveness through Make in India.** India's manufacturing sector has not grown rapidly and there is needed to accelerate growth in this sector to about 12 per cent per year from the current average of 8 per cent per year. We have dynamic entrepreneurship and with foreign assistance, we would be able to enhance the growth rate.

- **Development of Communications and associated structures.** The most important constraint in achieving a faster growth of manufacturing is the fact that infrastructure consisting of roads, railways, ports, airports, communications and power is not up to international standards. This must be substantially rectified if our enterprises are to compete effectively. Indian industry recognises increasingly open trading environment and no longer expects to survive due to protection. Countries like the US, China and Japan benefit from state of the art infrastructure. A co-terminus approach combining civil and military needs will serve the needs of rapid mobilisation and sustained logistics. The current government is working hard in this field.

- **Protecting the Environment.** Environmental concerns will affect our industry in the long run. The taming of Brahmaputra by the Chinese and the disputes over the Indus Water Treaty have tremendous significance. Economic development will be beneficial in the long term if environmental checks are undertaken.

Sustainable Energy. India needs to ensure the following towards ensuring sustained energy supply:

- Sustainable energy supply is vital for India's Comprehensive National Development and national security. By 2030, India will be approximately 90 per cent dependent on energy imports—a critical national vulnerability. India would compete with China and to a lesser extent with Pakistan and other South Asian states over energy resources. Further domination of SLOCs in the Indian Ocean Region (IOR) would be essential to ensure the smooth flow of oil and deter other players from exercising strategic coercion or resort to military intimidation.

- On the energy issue, three hard truths confront our decision makers. The first is the demand for energy is surging. The second aspect pertains to the fact that domestic supplies are struggling to keep pace and the third the environment is under stress. These three realities need to be tackled in the context of fluctuating price and supply vulnerabilities as also concerns about the safety of nuclear energy.
- The following measures are recommended in order to ensure energy security:
  - Diversify the energy resources from alternate markets like Central Asia, Africa and Latin America.
  - Exploring prospects for forging energy cooperation with the regional players and other energy-rich nations. It is important for India to be present in the energy scene by involving in upstream and downstream activities.
  - Since tankers meet our operational needs, it is necessary to enhance shipping and port infrastructure to match energy imports. It is of equal importance to ensure the safety and security of shipping and pipelines.
  - With the recent signing of the basic agreements, there is a need to operationalise the nuclear deal at the earliest.
  - India would need the credible military capability to protect its offshore energy assets, navigate without coercion in the international waters and ensure the protection of SLOCs.

Water Security. India would need large quantities of water by 2030. In order to ensure water security the following is recommended:

- Besides water conservation and harvesting, India should expeditiously link its rivers and canals in a national grid and ensure equitable distribution of water to various states.
- Leverage the Indus Water Treaty against Pakistan by seeking renegotiation of water sharing. If Pakistan becomes a failed state, run by a rabid anti-India regime, then this would compel Pakistan to moderate its behaviour to India.
- Resolve Teesta water sharing with Bangladesh to earn goodwill and consolidate pro-India sentiment in that country.

- Encourage and assist Nepal to harness the potential of its rivers flowing into India to generate electricity and earn revenue by supplying it to India. Nepal should be persuaded to take a leaf from Indo-Bhutan hydropower cooperation.
- India should build an opinion along with Bangladesh and other countries to urge China to sign the UN Convention on water sharing and become a responsible stakeholder in the sharing of global commons.

Politico-Diplomatic Measures

Internal Focus

In India, domestic geopolitics play an important role in the conduct of foreign policy. The issues that merit consideration are fiery debates over 123 Nuclear Agreement, foreign direct investment in the retail sector, resolution of disputes on the border settlement, water sharing, illegal migrants from Bangladesh and the Tamil ethnicity factor in bilateral relations with Sri Lanka. Regional issues are important and playing a larger role in the formulation of our foreign policy. There is a need to evolve an in house consultative mechanism to ensure that the legitimate concerns of the state are addressed before undertaking a foreign policy initiative.

India's vibrant electronic and social media play an important role in shaping public perceptions. Often they hijack foreign policy agenda causing embarrassment to our government. The Public Diplomacy Division at the Ministry of External Affairs needs to engage proactively with all sections of media to sponsor and steer good discussions on India's foreign policy forays thus managing discord and building public consensus.

Shortage of diplomatic cadre and inadequate focus on multi-disciplinary approach in the conduct of foreign policy pose constraints in the proactive conduct of diplomacy. The diplomatic cadre must be trained to be able to handle emerging challenges effectively. Towards adopting a multi-disciplinary approach it is recommended that a Group or Coordination committee be established comprising specialists, diplomats and selected military officers who are trained in defence cooperation to conceptualise, plan and conduct important projects in a time bound manner. These measures will enhance our credibility in terms of deliverance particularly in the eyes of our neighbours.

External Focus

Geopolitical and strategic centrality affords India excellent opportunities to create an India-centric South Asia and consolidate its influence for playing a bigger role in the strategic neighbourhood. India should consolidate its influence and emerge as a net security provider, a fulcrum of regional economic integration and as a lucrative socio-political and economic role model for South Asian states. India should remain cognizant of China's strategic forays into South Asia and the potential to induce a gravitational pull to wean away these countries into the Chinese orbit. A pro-China tilt in South Asian countries will be inimical to India's interests. The Central theme of our foreign policy in the regional periphery should be to seek congruence between legitimate aspirations of each country with India's abiding strategic objectives. These are Successful conduct of India's Act East Policy, Connect Central Asia Policy, Pre-eminence in the Indian Ocean Region and preserving strategic autonomy should be the main pillars of our foreign policy. To this end some of the foreign policy goals are as elucidated below:

Military Diplomacy

Due to lack of substantial trust and goodwill, Indian neighbours have employed military diplomacy with China. China's involvement in military affairs of South Asia is a worrying sign for India. There are two ways for India to tackle this. The first would be to enhance India's military diplomacy with Chinese neighbours. This would imply to increase military contact with Chinese neighbours like Vietnam, Japan, South Korea and the Philippines. This would be a Quid Pro Quo to heighten China's insecurity in its backyard. The second aspect would be India needs to intensify its military diplomacy in South Asia as well. A South Asian Defence University could be set up in India to enhance military contact in the region. Military conferences, joint maritime patrolling, disaster management exercises, anti-terrorism exercises, and military sports are some of the areas which India must build with its South Asian neighbours.

South Asian Economic Integration

Economic integration helps member countries in maintaining a united position in different platforms reduces armed conflicts and results in greater sharing of knowledge and culture. However, efforts made until now in this direction have not yielded desirable results. Barring Afghanistan, Nepal and Bhutan all the South Asian economies depend heavily on markets outside the region. Pakistan has been an irritant in the efforts for South Asian economic integration. India's trade with other neighbours is good but it still has the potential for more. It is high time that India starts contemplating about South Asian economic integration without Pakistan. The likeminded countries should be pursued and brought together for regional trade. Issues like the development of transport facilities, infrastructure, time-bound customs clearance, harmonisation of documentation and dispute settlement period should be taken care of leading to effective regional economic integration.

Sanctity of Strategic Buffers

India's focus should be to consolidate its influence in Bhutan and Nepal. These countries border strategically important Siliguri corridor which is a vital link to the North Eastern states which have borders with China, Bangladesh and Myanmar. Security of this corridor is crucial for India's strategic security and success of Act East Policy. Creeping influence of China in Bhutan, Nepal and Bangladesh will perpetuate India's security concerns both in terms of traditional and nontraditional threats. The recent Doklam incident bears testimony to this aspect.

Bangladesh

The present Awami League regime under Sheikh Hasina has been extremely friendly to India. India has resolved the Border issue and now must resolve the Teesta River dispute amicably to enable connectivity between West Bengal and the North Eastern states. Further great scope exists in boosting trade and defence cooperation between the countries. Bangladesh is actively cooperating in preventing militants operating from their country.

China

India and China are destined by geography to be neighbours and share the same strategic space for resources, locations and influence. Historical evidence suggests that a country with strong CNP acquires hegemonic outlook and China is no exception. At the same time, India cannot allow herself to be coerced or intimidated by China. Multi-dimensional engagement at one level as also developing and leveraging credible deterrence at another should be the cornerstone of India's China policy.

Measures Suggested in Engaging and Deterring China

Economic Engagement and Cooperation

- Bilateral trade with China has crossed $ 84 billion and is poised to reach $ 100 billion shortly. This has the potential to rise further.
- Currently, China seeks bigger investments in Indian markets and infrastructure sector. China's economic forays into Indian markets should be calibrated and balanced by similar access to Indian enterprises by Mainland China.
- India needs to address the issue of skewed trade balance (2/3 in China's favour). While India needs to enhance its investments in the pharmaceuticals and software sectors in China, more fields should be explored to bridge the gap.
- China has evinced interest in boosting trade with India along Nathula-Kalimpong-Siliguri-Kolkata corridor. Other potential trade corridors between the two countries could be Myanmar-Bangladesh-India, along with the River Sutlej in Himachal, Demchok (Ladakh) to Xinjiang, via Chabahar-Afghanistan-Central Asia-Xinjiang or along the North-South corridor which intersects the East-West Eurasian corridor. India must keep her diplomatic options open to discuss these issues at Track 2 level to gauge China's response.
- Enhanced cooperation at the World Trade Organisation, Brazil Russia, India, China summit and Shanghai Cooperation Organisation.
- The two countries should set up Joint Working Groups on Intelligence Sharing with regard to Jihadi networks.
- China acknowledges India as an old civilisation Worthy of a dialogue.

India–China–US–Japan Equation

Given China's profound perception of grand encirclement, India's growing strategic partnership with the US and Japan will be viewed with concern. This could either nudge China to be more accommodative to adopt a hardened approach towards India. India on her part needs to exhibit a high degree of statecraft to maintain balance. Subtle politics diplomatic signaling should demonstrate to China the range of strategic options India could exercise if its strategic interests are not heeded.

Resolving the Border Issue between India and China

The operative agreements and mechanisms such as the Border Peace and Tranquility Agreement of 1993, Confidence Building Measures of 1996, Guiding Principles of 2005, the Working Mechanism for Consultation and Coordination of 2012 and recently Border Defence Cooperation Agreement exist between India and China to negotiate on their Border Dispute. Nonetheless, China continues to use the border dispute as a pressure point against India. Creeping assertiveness at the border and engineering incidents like Daulat Beg Oldie (DBO) are timed to convey a political message and test India's resolve and response. The Border issue remains a potential flashpoint between the two countries. The following are recommended:

- India must develop Quid Pro Quo capabilities at the LAC and enhance its abilities from Dissuasion to Deterrence.
- Infrastructure must be built and upgraded. Force accretions must be undertaken and voids filled up.
- India's sensitivity over the illegal cessation of Shaksgam Valley by Pakistan to China in 1963 and Chinese presence in the Northern Areas which legally belong to India should be emphatically flagged at diplomatic talks and the issues must be kept alive.

Exploiting China's Multi-Front Dilemma

The US security alliances in the Asia Pacific, its Asian pose multi-front dilemma for China. The US, Japan, Vietnam, South Korea perceive India as a Strategic swing state and acknowledge her as an important stakeholder in the region. From India's strategic perspective, China needs to be kept embroiled in the western Pacific imbroglio. China's preoccupation in the East China Sea and South China Sea will provide India with the much desired time window to narrow the power asymmetry. Special emphasis should be laid on strong and multi-layered defence ties with Japan, Vietnam, Philippines and South Korea. At the same time, India should join collaborative Security mechanisms for protection of SLOCs and critical infrastructure against all forms of threat as this would become important for India's movement of energy requirements. The following is recommended:

- India should show the flag in the East China Sea and the South China Sea. She should participate in bilateral and Multilateral exercises to demonstrate her capability and resolve of accessing the global commons and demonstrating her resolve to navigate in international waters. Specific focus should be over securing arrangement for birthing and basing of ships as also institutionalise conduct of exercises with Vietnam and Japan. Quad should be strengthened.

- While China-Taiwan relations have improved considerably, India continues to shy away from a strategic engagement with Taiwan. India must entice Taiwan to invest in India's communications sector. Cooperation in the fields of education and youth exchange programme such as the National Cadet Corps must be exploited.

- Xinjiang and Tibet, these non-Han provinces are China's greatest vulnerability and thus need to be seen as pressure points. China already stands isolated in the eyes of the international community. For oppressing the sub-national movements and for violating human rights. India needs to develop subtle leverages with Uighur diaspora and re-energise linkages with the Tibetan resistance. This would act as a quid pro quo should coercion and abetment of anti-national activities in India. Tibetans and Uighurs can be India's best Human Intelligence resources inside China. They can provide real-time intelligence and facilitate operations by Special Forces and Special Frontier Forces.

National Security

Reforms in National Security Architecture

Our national security apparatus needs to be made more responsive to current threats. It must be made operationally ready to meet a broad spectrum of hybrid and asymmetric security threats. It must be geared to meet the challenges of modern-day warfare. The modernisation of the Armed Forces needs to be expedited. Reforms suggested by Kargil Committee, Arun Singh Committee, Group of Ministers and Naresh Chandra Committee have not been fully implemented due to frivolous political calculations or at the behest of the bureaucratic establishment that favours status quo. There is a need to institutionalise a system of parliamentary committees like in the Western countries to make vision document (Transformation Vision 2030) for the long term modernization of the security apparatus. There is a requirement to form Armed Forces Committees, Technology Commission, Space

Commission, Maritime Commission and others to prepare vision documents, transformation roadmaps and then oversee their importance.

The National Security Council, National Security Advisory Board, Strategic Planning Division and the newly formed Defence Planning Committee are the apex institutions dealing with security at the highest level. However structurally and functionally these organisations have not been able to optimise their functioning to make India's security responsive. There is a need to review their mandate, organisational structures, the composition of the functionaries and the very system of their modus operandi. There is a need to induct high calibre civil servants, diplomats, academicians, members of strategic community, police and the armed forces to transform these organisations into multi speciality entities capable of producing documents like National Security Strategy, Strategic Defence Review and such like other vision documents.

Modifying Rules of Business

Government of India Allocation of Business Rules and the Government of India Transaction of Business Rules framed in 1961 under the constitutional powers of the President of India should be reviewed and reframed. As per present rules, it is the Defence Minister, who is assigned the responsibility of defence of India. The three Service Chiefs who are important stakeholders in the national security should be accorded a befitting status and power in the security edifice of the Government of India. They should be consulted on all security matters.

Jointness among the Services

In order to increase the much desired Jointness between the Ministry of Defence and the Service HQs as also within the Services cross-posting of military officers of the rank of two stars and below/Joint Secretary.

Appointment of Chief of Defence Staff

Under the new dispensation, the Service Chiefs should continue to exercise command and control over the three services. The Chief of Defence Staff, on the other hand, should be the Permanent Chairman Chief of Staff Committee and he should exercise direct command over the following:

- Andaman and Nicobar Command.
- Strategic Forces Command.
- Cyber Command.
- Space Command.
- Logistics Command.
- Joint Doctrine and Training Command.
- Out of Area Contingency Task Force. (The last five are under consideration).

He should also be consulted by the Defence Minister and by the Cabinet Committee on Security on important tri-services and national security issues. HQ Integrated Defence Services should be strengthened and should undertake seminal work to prepare joint military doctrine, joint military strategy as well as doctrines on Asymmetric and Information Warfare. They should conceptualise, plan and conduct strategic game exercises to train and rehearse the National Command Authority and its staff on strategic security scenarios, management of escalation domination as also control. Further, they must plan and conduct tri-service military exercises.

The theatre commands of the three services and unified commands should be networked in terms of evolving joint theatre strategies, operational plans and conduct of joint military exercises. This issue is under serious consideration. All Agencies except the Indian Air Force have agreed to the establishment of Theatre Commands. It is a matter of time before the same is resolved.

Streamlining National Security Planning Process

India's strategic planning needs to graduate from linear thinking to undertaking a 360-degree horizon scan. This would be based on the process of 'Net Assessment' and 'Scenario Building'. The Planning Staff in the Services HQ and various Ministries should also be imparted formal training in this field. With regard to perspective planning in the Services, a seven-step approach needs to be adopted. Details as appended below:

- **Stage 1:** Articulation of a National Security Strategy. This is the Starting Point of the process. This broad-based document must draw inspiration from national core values and interests as also provide guidelines to various ministries to formulate their policies and evolve their strategies. This must be approved by the Cabinet Committee on Security.

- **Stage 2**: Formulation of Defence Planning Guidelines. The National Security Strategy will set the stage for the formulation of these guidelines which would address the National Aim, National Security Interests, National Security Objectives and other impellers of defence policy. The document leads to the specifics of the National Defence Strategy as well as the National Military Strategy.
- **Stage 3**: Formulation of a Defence Capability Strategy. Formulation of this document will identify the capabilities required for the assigned role of the armed forces. It would also suggest as to how the forces intend to provide a flexible suite of capabilities within the financial outlay and governmental priorities.
- **Stage 4**: Preparation of a Defence Capability Plan. Defence Capability Plan would be the road map for the development of future capabilities of armed forces over a fifteen years horizon.
- **Stage 5**: Preparation of Long Term Integrated Perspective Plan. The end product of the whole process would be this plan which would span over three five year plans. These plans should be finalised at Headquarters Integrated Defence Staff and not merely stitched together without any meaningful intervention. This should be approved by the Cabinet Committee of Security to ensure assured budgetary allocation. The Force Restructuring must aim at building up a viable capability-based force. This entails right sizing and reengineering. Multi-Role Task Forces should be built by Save and Raise. As any substantial increase in the defence budget is unlikely.
- **Stage 6**: Preparation of Joint Military Strategy. The Armed Forces should shed off their Service biases and sincerely work towards the formulation of comprehensive joint military strategy at the national and theatre level. Once a joint military strategy is in place, the allocation, control, employment of resources during a campaign and perspective planning for force development will get streamlined.
- **Stage 7**: Approach to Force Structure and Development. Our military planning continues to be Pakistani centric and there is a need to focus on China. It would be worthwhile to undertake a joint services study to identify the optimum combat resources needed to deter Pakistan and rebalance resources so that the primary focus is on the India China

border. The current deployment of the Strike and pivot Corps including the under raising Mountain Corps to be examined de novo. Further, a formation at the Corps level is reconfigured for a dual role and be located in the higher regions of Central India. Infrastructure is built to move this formation by rail and air.

Defence Expenditure

India's defence expenditure has not been in tune with strategic security needs. China's defence spending is approximately five times higher than that of India. The Armed Forces need a Defence Budget which is a minimum of 2.5 per cent to 3 per cent of GDP with an assured annual increase of 14.5 per cent. It must be realised that great asymmetry already exists between India and China in defence spending and military modernization. Truncated budget allocations will make this asymmetry unimaginable in the coming decade. It is obvious that if defence allocations are not increased, asymmetry in the defence capability vis-a-vis China will increase to unacceptable levels.

Development of Roads, Airfields and Other Infrastructures

There is a definite need to improve our infrastructure to face the Chinese challenge. Inadequacies in critical infrastructure, construction of multiple axes of induction, forward airfields, advanced landing grounds, helipads, gun areas, defence works, habitat, communication and logistics nodes should be built on a war footing. A great deal of synergy is required between State Governments, various Ministries at the Centre, particularly within the Ministry of Defence. Special dispensations must be given for completion of infrastructure projects in the larger interest of National Security. There is a need to strengthen the Border Roads Organization with other civilian agencies for expediting infrastructure development. Infrastructure in border areas will enhance tourism, boost the local economy and help in the integration of people from these regions with the mainstream of our country.

Indigenisation of Defence Industry

China has been able to leverage the advantage of defence industry by building extensive international linkages. Its arms exports have helped it in gaining significant inroads, particularly in Africa, South East Asia and countries of

South Asia. India urgently needs to focus on developing its defence industry and export arms to its neighbouring countries to gain goodwill, influence and leverages. Our lack of ability to produce and export arms is our weakest area and there is no pride in being the largest importer of arms in the world. Heavy import dependence of military hardware lends our nation vulnerable to corruption, coercion and arm twisting. Greater focus needs to be laid on the indigenisation of Research and Development as also defence production. Institutionalised integration of Services, Defence Research Development and Organisation as also civil industry is another area which needs immediate attention. The Private sector should be involved in building up the required technologies as we have a large pool of skilled manpower. In the interim, until our defence industry comes of age, we should explore the feasibilities of inviting foreign firms to set up defence industries in India under a joint and collaborative framework. This would boost the Make in India initiative which is the current mantra of the Indian Government. The new DPP 2016 would assist in this regard.

Technology

Technology will play an important role in any form of conflict in the coming decades. It is suggested that a "Defence Technology Commission" be set up to oversee technology development for the Armed Forces, This Commission may work through various panels or task forces comprising a mix of experienced scientists, technologists, officers of the Armed Forces, consultants from the industry, Research and Development, academia and the strategic community. Each service should set up its own design department like the Indian Navy and open their lines of communications with the scientific and industrial communities. It is heartening to see the Indian Army open its Defence Bureau. This is bound to result in positive development. The harnessing of scientific talent and allocation of more funds for Research & Development is necessary to reduce the country's dependence on technology imports.

Deterrence Capabilities. India needs to develop the following capabilities:

Intelligence, Surveillance and Reconnaissance

- There is a major need to upgrade capabilities in this field. Redundancy in Communications and surveillance satellites with sub meter resolution and daily revisit with Direct Downloading Facility at the Corps level should be accorded Top Priority.

- Development of viable signal and human intelligence capability to obtain reliable intelligence on China. The strategic Intelligence, Surveillance and Reconnaissance capability should be complemented by deploying state of the art reconnaissance aircraft and UAV with the live streaming facility at the surveillance centres at the national, theatre and sectoral levels.

- A Long Range Reconnaissance and Observation and Hand-Held Thermal Imaging tactical surveillance grid should be established along the border with the live streaming facility at the formation HQ up the chain of command.

- The Air Force should enhance its radar coverage on the mountainous border with China.

- Special attention to upgrading the maritime surveillance capability in the Indian Ocean Region.

Warning Time: The Research and Analysis Wing, diplomatic missions, National Technical Research Organisation and Defence Intelligence Agency should enhance their capability to constantly assess China's capability-intention matrix and provide a minimum of three months warning period to the National Command Authority as also Armed Forces for effecting an orderly mobilisation and implementation of surge plans. Indian Armed Forces should be prepared to undertake military operations under a truncated warning period since the indicators about the enemy's intentions about the enemy's intentions and build up will be diffused and mixed. Contingency plans for a graduated mobilisation and trickle in logistics build up should be prepared and rehearsed. A major consideration in this regard should be to posture forces in areas where they can be acclimatised before speedy induction into operational areas.

Targeting

- There is need to induct on priority long-range precision-guided weapon systems for a key point, in-depth strikes, long-range multi-barrel rocket launchers, BrahMos with long range (600 km) steep dive capability, air superiority fighters supported by Airborne Warning and Control

Systems and air to air refuelers. Precision Guided Munitions must be inducted by the three Services.

- The artillery needs Medium Guns and they need to be procured and inducted. Ultra-Light Howitzers would be an excellent piece of equipment for all-terrain and Out of Area Contingencies. The current deal must be finalised.

- Aerospace and Special Forces capability should be developed to target Chinese assets at Kyakphu and Gwadar. They should also be directed on the container conveys along Sittwe-Kunming highway and along Karakoram highway. Creation of such capabilities would also act to enhance the cost of intervention for China.

- Fail-safe multiple means of communication are vital for the sensor-shooter interface. With these capabilities in place, India can impede and degrade the Chinese build up in Tibetan plateau and in the Indian Ocean.

Land Forces: Modernisation in the Army should be as under:

- Early operationalisation of Mountain Strike Corps (two mountain divisions, three armoured brigades, three Artillery Brigades, one Air Defence brigade and one Aviation Brigade).

- Need for a review at force structuring. Considering the terrain there would be a need for two additional strike Corps to undertake offensive capability in Ladakh. Sikkim and Arunachal sectors. The current boards regarding the right sizing of the Army are geared to optimisation of manpower but force structure needs to be modified.

- The Pivot and Strike Corps on the Western Border to be restructured into integrated mission oriented battle groups.

- Restructure infantry formations deployed in the mountains and provide them with surveillance, communications, tactical mobility and firepower capabilities. Each division in the Indian Army must have a squadron of UCAVs.

- Remove existing hollowness of the Indian Army. Procure and induct UAVs, Medium Guns, Tank ammunition, night vision devices, precision-guided munitions, Air Defence Systems to include Quick Reaction Surface to Air Missile and Spike Anti-Tank Guided Missiles.

- Army Aviation Wing to be expanded.

- Induction of steep dive BrahMos supersonic Cruise missile on the Sino Indian border with a range of 600 km.

Maritime Capability: SLOCs in the Arabian Sea, Bay of Bengal and the Indian Ocean are China's critical vulnerability. India must enhance its maritime capability to interdict SLOCs and choke the strategic straits. India needs to augment the capabilities of the Andaman and Nicobar Command as also Western, Eastern Naval and Air Force Commands to execute such tasks. The Indian submarine fleet must be equipped and trained in undertaking offensive stealth missions against Chinese Vulnerable Areas and Vulnerable Points on its Eastern Seaboard. Even if not used for launching attacks, this would put tremendous psychological pressure on the PLAN. Our own Navy's capability to dominate the Straits of Hormuz, Bab-el-Mandeb and Malacca should be augmented with the following:

- Besides the aircraft carrier modernization focus should be to develop Helicopter based Carriers, Cruisers, Destroyers and Frigates with Anti Air and Anti-Submarine capabilities.
- Strategic nuclear capability should be enhanced by inducting state of the art Submersible Ship Nuclear submarine and, Submersible Ship Ballistic Missile Nuclear Submarines. Further conventional submarines must have the capability of firing nuclear missiles. The feasibility of induction of mini-submarines or mini submersible vehicles for stealth warfare should be developed.
- The current acquisition of Boeing P8 I Long Range Maritime Reconnaissance planes provides our Navy with the capability to mount surveillance beyond the traditional sphere of influence. Our Naval Air station in Great Nicobar island as also the acquisition of Rotary UAVs and Light Combat Aircraft will enhance our effectiveness to undertake surveillance of the Eastern region. It would be prudent to develop Lakshadweep into a forward naval base. The Naval Aviation will enhance its capability with the MIG 29K and multi-role helicopters.
- Our amphibious capability needs to be enhanced to the landing of a division with additional landing platform docks.
- Andaman and Nicobar Command should be upgraded in terms of surveillance and targeting with deployment of modern frigates, fast patrol combatant vessels, UAVs and deployment of Sukhoi 30s.

- The Indian Ocean Navy Symposium and Exercise Milan must be leveraged to constructively engage regional navies.

Aerospace: The Prime Minister of India has ensured that the Rafale deal has been finalised. Other issues to be initiated are as under:

- Early induction of indigenously manufactured aircraft Tejas, a joint production of Fifth Generation Fighter Aircraft between Russia and India and state of the art Attack helicopters.
- All weather radar coverage to include Aerostats.
- Airborne Early Warning and Control, Embraer based system for Command and Control function. The need to complete the procurement of Chinook Heavy Lift helicopter as also the optimisation of Mi-17 V variants in our operational environment.
- Induction of air refuellers of Airbus A 330 MRTT.
- Upgrading of airfields and construction of new Advanced Landing Grounds in the Eastern theatre, Ladakh and Andaman & Nicobar.
- Our land-based Surface to Air Missile system defences to be based on Akash and Spyder or any other state of the art system.

Air Defence: Currently, this is our critical weakness and merits immediate attention. Inadequate Air Defence capability against the Chinese Second Artillery and PLAFF's air superiority fighters is another grey area. There is a need to optimise the deployment of Air Defence resources of the three Services and streamline the Integrated Control and Reporting System. It is heartening to note the induction of S 400 weapon system.

A Pocket of Excellence Forces: India needs to develop asymmetric capabilities through the following measures:

- In addition to nuclear weapons, India should develop anti-satellite weapons, laser weapons, Electro Magnetic Pulse missiles, microwave and other thermal and kinetic energy weapons. All modern armies are developing weapons with such disruptive technologies. A case in point is the secret 'Assassins Mace Weapons Programme' of China. India should invest in such a weapons system.
- Military applications for Outer Space must be developed. With our capability to reach Mars, our focus must be on future applications to

include weapon systems as also weapons to defend and destroy space-based systems.

- There is a need to have an advanced Intelligence, Surveillance and Reconnaissance capability over Tibet Autonomous Region. Further, there must be a daily revisit of satellite surveillance capability with Direct Downloading Capability at the Corps level. Over the Horizon Radars need to be linked to having better inputs regarding targets.
- Higher priority should be given to developing space-based C^4I^2SR, guidance and navigation systems operating in the optical, infrared and microwave realms of the spectrum.
- Cyber warfare units should be raised. Electronic Warfare and Information Warfare capability should be enhanced to conduct network-centric operations.

Strategic Mobility: In a two front scenario, it is imperative that the National Command Authority makes an early decision to decide its flank of operation. A quick decision would enable early move and induction of Dual Task Formation from one front to another. The Air Force as also the Civil Aviation assets must tailor their strategic transport fleet for effecting the rapid mobilisation of Rapid Reaction Forces. A great deal of coordination is also needed with the Railways for ensuring speedy mobilisation of formations at short notice. The Special Forces personnel should be sent to countries of interest for the area and cultural familiarisation trips. The Special Forces and Special Frontier Forces should also be tasked to create a rear security dilemma in the enemy territory.

Employment of Special Forces: The Special Forces of the three services should be integrated under the Special Forces Command and there should be better coordination between the Special Forces and Special Frontier Forces. These forces must be equipped with state of the art equipment, trained in multi-skills, mandated and employed for strategic tasks within and beyond Indian Borders.

Out of Area Contingency: India should consider raising a Tri-service Joint Task Force (JTF) to cater for out of area contingencies such as Kandahar crisis, intervention in the Maldives and for rendering humanitarian assistance during conflicts or disasters and projection of power. The Joint Task Force could also be used with our sovereign space for a host of operational contingencies which warrant a rapid military response. The Joint Task Force could also be a nodal agency for the conduct of multilateral training with foreign armed forces.

Nuclear Capabilities: In order to build credible strategic deterrence, the following measures are recommended:

- India should develop a triad based nuclear deterrence capability. This should, in addition, ensure the ability to absorb a nuclear strike and thereafter deliver a second strike. To make the Indian deterrence credible there is a need to undertake the following:
  - Operationalise Agni V. Test the Agni VI with an ICBM capability.
  - Develop thermonuclear warheads.
  - Develop Multiple Independently targetable Re-entry Vehicle and Manoeuverable Re-entry Vehicle.
  - Operationalise nuclear submarines in greater quantities with nuclear missiles both in ballistic and Cruise Mode.
  - Concurrently Ballistic Missile Defence capability should be developed to protect major communication centres, strategic assets and the National Command Authority. Induct S 400 effectively. We must refine our existing ASAT capability.
  - Our current "No First Use Policy" needs to be reviewed. Nuclear brinkmanship is a mind game targeted at the political leadership and the people of a target country. The Indian nuclear doctrine should reflect the resolve to use nuclear weapons when our vital interests or survival is at stake. The doctrine needs to be reviewed.

Integrated Theatre Logistics: This would entail the integration of resources of the three services, civil government and non-government agencies. A model that is dynamic, flexible, based on forwarding delivery and plug and play system should be introduced. It should cater to the logistics needs of pivot formations and accretion forces including the Para Military Forces.

Rear Area Security: Military doctrines of Pakistan and China advocate the continuous harassment of the adversary from the rear. In order to impede Indian mobilisation, the adversary is expected to use non-state or agent provocateurs to target communications arteries and harass our forces. Our

Rear Area Security schemes remain ad-hoc and the Central Armed Police Forces are neither equipped nor trained or rehearsed to accomplish this important role. The issue demands great ministerial attention.

Role of Central Armed Police and Para Military Force: There is a considerable mismatch in the equipment profile, training, professional ethos, system of functioning, Command and Control of Border Security Force, Indo Tibetan Border Police and Assam Rifles. A case in point is that the Indo Tibetan Border Police deployed on the India China border is not under operational control of the Army. These organisations form an essential part of the defensive layout and have a crucial role in our design of battle. These forces should be restructured on the lines of infantry units and placed under operational control of the Army for training, operational preparedness and deployment in operational areas. In order to ensure integration, synergy, command and control as also operational effectiveness these organisations must be placed under the Ministry of Defence while operating with the Army.

Defensive Capability: In order to augment the defence preparedness, the following should be considered:

- The Army should carry out an objective operational preparedness audit of its defensive capability to discern, delay, disrupt and defeat the enemy's build up. Critical operational voids, including pre-fabricated and tailor, made defence works should be made on Top Priority.
- Surge plans in the event of a Chinese attack should be identified and rehearsed realistically. Further weaknesses should be identified and addressed in a time-bound manner.
- China has an adequate number of formations for offensive operations in Ladakh and Sikkim sector. There is a need to augment anti-tank potential of infantry units, enhance medium gun densities, and allocate air resources for effective degradation battle. There is a need to induct mechanised forces in strength in these areas. A light tank for the mountains must be trial evaluated.
- Formations should be earmarked, structured and trained for rapid response at the division as also at the Corps level.
- Defence of Arunachal Pradesh less the Kameng Division and Eastern

Ladakh should be accorded highest priority in achieving optimum defence preparedness.

- Defensive posture in the sensitive Akhnoor, Poonch, Uri and Kargil should be strengthened to deny Pakistan Army from altering the alignment of the LOC in Jammu and Kashmir.
- Defence of Vulnerable Areas and Vulnerable Points in the coastal belt against all forms of threats including terrorist strikes should be ensured.
- Defence of island territories, particularly isolated islands in Andaman and Nicobar should be reviewed and strengthened against all forms of threat including Non-State Actors.

Offensive Capability: A potent offensive capability is an inescapable imperative which is necessary to capture sensitive enemy territory and leverage this for resolution of conflict on favourable terms. The following is recommended:

- There are a number of sectors which lend themselves for a swift offensive towards Chinese operational centres of gravity. While strengthening our defences in vulnerable sectors, the focus should be to develop launch pads and pre-emptively posture own offensive formations opposite China's vulnerable sectors. These moves can effectively deter the opponent from undertaking any military misadventure and also to provide own side options to take the battle into enemy territory.
- The mountain strike formations should be tailored as composite, mission-oriented battle groups, equipped with light equipment, lethal firepower and capable of operating in small subunits at successive depths of enemy's defensive layout. The strike formations should excel in manoeuvre attacks and indirect approach in mountainous terrain.
- Capability for the employment of mechanised and heli mobile forces for the offensive should be developed.
- Specialised units should be organised, equipped, trained and tasked for special reconnaissance and harassing tasks behind the enemy lines at tactical depth including defensive formations.
- The troops should be trained to fight in hostile nuclear and Electronic Warfare environment.
- In case of a two-front war the capability must exist for operations against both China and Pakistan to complement conventional strikes with Non-contact covert operations.

- Develop strong Anti-Access, Area Denial in Tibet and Indian Ocean Region. This could be undertaken by using our Aerospace resources and the Indian Navy.
- Maritime and Aerospace capabilities are used to dominate strategic choke points in the Indian Ocean Region.

Offensive Outlook: India is perceived as a pacifist and a country that believes in the status quo. This image needs to be changed across the political, diplomatic and military spectrum. A deliberate effort is needed to develop dynamism, pro-active approach and an offensive mindset in our leadership. Linear thinking should be replaced by a 360 degrees view, shedding conservatism and predictability syndrome. The approach to strategic security should be based on objective assessment and a comprehensive strategic response. Our current surgical strikes against Pakistan are a step in the right direction.

Developing the Art of Public Diplomacy

Wars are won or lost in the minds of a country's national leadership which gets influenced by domestic and international public perceptions. Efforts must be made to shed India's pacifist image of a soft state which is a reluctant global player. Sound psychological and information operational themes should be propagated through diplomacy, Diaspora, media and cyberspace. This should be combined with credible demonstration of soft and hard power which should project India's political will to respond effectively for safeguarding national interests. Proactive defence diplomacy in the form of joint military exercises, exchange of delegations, the conduct of symposiums, demonstration of military capabilities, export of weapons have the most direct and visible effect in shaping perceptions.

India should raise information and psychological warfare units comprising experts from a different discipline. Special effort should be made to educate Indian media on security matters. Theme based media campaigns should be undertaken to build political and public consensus on India's vital national interests, strategic objectives and policy options for dealing with intricate and vexed issues such as the resolution of the border. Publication and circulation of White Papers, Strategic Defence Reviews and literature on security issues is yet another way of shaping perceptions and portraying India's contemporary strategic culture.

India has traditionally been showcasing its military capabilities by undertaking joint military exercises and undertaking firepower demonstrations in the western border. Similar military events should be conducted in plains of West Bengal, Assam and Ladakh where the diplomatic community to include military observers and the media should be invited. Theme based media publicity should be given to these events. There is a need to develop expertise in undertaking high pitched propaganda in South Asia, ASEAN, European Union and United Nations in keeping with our overall information strategy.

Developing Nodes of Excellence on China

India's perceptions of China are based on incomplete understanding and reflect the bruised psyche from the 1962 war as also from motivated Western opinion and perspective. India cannot ignore the requirement of developing its own insight into China. We need to invest and create China specialists who are not only conversant with the Chinese language but those who are capable of analysing Chinese literature, interacting with Chinese think tanks. Further, they are also well conversed with operational dynamics. HQ Integrated Defence Staff and Service HQ should create their own China Study Centres comprising of reputed members of the strategic community. Academicians, retired diplomats, military professionals and selected Services officers. These study groups should regularly interact with think tanks in India and abroad and prepare comprehensive assessments as also policy papers for decision makers. These efforts will go a long way in developing a better understanding of China and calibrating our strategic response to his modernisation programme.

Summary of Conclusions

By 2030, China would have a modern Army, a Blue Water Navy and an Air Force capable of dominating airspace in areas of conflict. Developments would also take place in Second Artillery (PLARF), Outer Space and Direct Energy weapons. China has also floated the concept of One Belt One Road which would improve China's connectivity with its extended neighbourhood. This modernisation is likely to result in great capabilities. Greater capabilities will lead to greater ambitions. Further, China is becoming assertive in its disputes with Taiwan, Japan, Vietnam, Philippines and India. This has to be responded by these countries as China is bound to have domestic problems like slowing down of its economic growth, which could be tranquilised by external arm twisting in demonstration of its military might against these countries.

The current trends indicate a rise in assertiveness be it declaration of ADIZ or the May 2014 placement of mobile oil rig by 80 PLAN ships with Air cover in the proximity of Paracel Islands resulting in a maritime standoff with Vietnam. Further, China has been reclaiming land and building airstrips in the South China Sea. India has undergone numerous transgressions, the last one being the incident in Doklam for 73 days from 16 June 2017 to 28 August 2017.

China has stated that the border dispute will take a long time to resolve. Its military modernisation and equipping of nuclear weapons to Pakistan pose a direct threat to India. Chinese capabilities by its modernisation enhance its abilities to launch a full spectrum offensive against India. India on its part being a democratic country is deliberate and needs more time to respond to PLA assertiveness and can't take any chances with reading of Chinese intentions. Accordingly, India has to be prepared for a full spectrum conflict with China by 2030.

A school of thought exists that nuclear weapons negate a major war between India and China. Even in such an eventuality limited wars and its modern variations cannot be ruled out. In such a case China is likely to use Cyber Warfare, Anti Satellite Weapons, Missiles, Overwhelming Firepower and possibly a Ground Offensive comprising multiple intrusions. This possibly calls for India to undertake measures elucidated below:

- Need for National Security Strategy and strategic response to China by intensification of strategic partnerships with the US, Japan, Vietnam, Australia and Russia.
- Build up our Comprehensive National Power.
- Joint operations in network-centric conditions.
- Modernise our Armed Forces to cater for the simultaneous threat from China and Pakistan with focus on a Blue Water Navy to cater for Asia Pacific region.
- Reorganise our DRDO to focus only on cutting edge technologies.
- Focus on development of Outer Space Technology for strategic purposes.

- Create a level playing field between Defence Public Sector Units and the private sector.
- Develop pockets of excellence by focusing on Asymmetric Warfare, Cyber Warfare and Assassins Mace Weapons.
- Create a diplomatic strategy to win the war as also peace.
- Work towards a strategic relationship with Taiwan.
- Deal with China pragmatically in trade, the building of infrastructure and other areas of cooperation.

*

Glossary

ABM. Anti-ballistic missile, designed to knock down incoming missiles or their warheads before designated targets are struck.

Asymmetric Warfare. Asymmetric Warfare is a term used to describe a military situation in which two belligerents of unequal power or capacity of action, interact and take advantage of their strength and weaknesses of themselves and their enemies. This interaction often involves strategies and tactics outside the realm of conventional warfare. It may include the use of cyber and information warfare and/or chemical, biological, radiological or nuclear-related technologies.

Information Warfare. It is the offensive or defensive use of information and systems to exploit corrupt or destroy an adversary's information and systems while protecting one's own. It is the emerging theatre in which future conflicts at the strategic level is most likely to occur,

Proxy War. It is a war conducted between nations utilising non-state players to fight on their behalf. The extent and support provided by the states will vary but financial and logistical support is normally provided.

Second Strike Capability. Ability to absorb a nuclear strike from the enemy and thereafter delivering a retaliatory blow with adequate nuclear weapons to destroy the enemy.

Second Artillery. This is the arm of the People's Liberation Army of China which operates missiles and rockets. These could be both nuclear and conventional. These under the recent reforms have been redesignated as Rocket Force as also Strategic Support Force.

Triad. Strategic weapons comprising of bombers, submarines and missiles capable of launching nuclear weapons from land. Sea and Air.

*

Bibliography

Arvind Gupta, Ajay Lele and Amitav Malik, "Space Security Need For Global Convergence," Pentagon Press, New Delhi, 2012.

Air Cmde Ramesh V Phadke, "Defending Indian Skies against the PLAAF", *Indian Defence Review*, January-March 2012, pp. 39-45.

C Raja Mohan, "Samudra Manthan", Carnegie Endowment for International Peace, United States,

Capt R K Shirohi, "Military Strength of China," Prashant Publishing House, Delhi-11094, 2011.

Colonel Qao Ling and Colonel Wang Siang Sui, "Unrestricted Warfare," Beijing PLA Literature and Arts Publishing House, 1999.

Dr Srikanth Kondapalli, "China's Military and India," Pentagon Press, New Delhi, 2012.

Gurmeet Kanwal, "The New Arthashastra", HarperCollins Publishers India, Sector 57, Noida, Uttar Pradesh 201301, India, 2016.

Gurmeet Kanwal, "Sharpening the Arsenal", HarperCollins Publishers India, Sector 57, Noida, Uttar Pradesh 201301, India, 2017.

Gurmeet Kanwal and Dhruv Katoch, "China's Defence Policy, Indian Perspective," KW Publishers Private Limited, New Delhi-110002, 2011.

Henry Kissinger, "On China", Penguin United Kingdom, 2012

I Chung Lai, "Prospects and Perspectives", Prospect Foundation, Taipei, Taiwan, Republic of China, 2016.

James Mulvenon, "Soldiers of Fortune," M E Sharpe, Armonk, New York-10504, 2001.

Laxman Behera and Vinay Kaushal, "Defence Acquisition; International Best Practices," Pentagon Press, New Delhi, 2013.

Lora Saalman, "Chinese Views on India's Ballistic Missile Defence," CLAWS, New Delhi, 2013.

Lt Gen A K Singh and Lt Gen B S Nagal, "Military Strategy for India in the 21st Century," KW Publishers Private Limited, New Delhi-110002, 2019.

Lt Gen C K Kapur, "Chinese Military Modernization," Manas Publications, New Delhi-110002, 2003.

Lt Gen Gautam Banerjee, "India's National Defence, Defining Defence Reforms and Military Modernisation", Pentagon Press, Shahpur Jat, New Delhi-110049, 2017.

Lt Gen J S Bajwa, "China Threat or Challenge", Lancer Publishers, Sarvapriya Vihar, New Delhi-110016, India, 2017.

Lt Gen J S Bajwa, "Modernisation of the Chinese PLA", Lancer Publishers, Sarvapriya Vihar, New Delhi-110016, India, 2013.

Michael Pillsbury, "China Debates the Future Security Environment," NDU Press, 2000.

Michael Pillsbury, "Chinese Views of Future Warfare, "NDU Press, 1998.

Monika Chansoria, "Military Modernization and Strategy", KW Publishers Private Limited, New Delhi, 2011.

Nan Li, "The PLA'S Evolving Campaign Doctrine and Strategies," RAND, Santa Monica, USA.

Peng Guanggion and Yao Youzhi, "The Science of Military Strategy," Military Science Publishing House, Beijing, 2005.

Ralph D. Sawyer, "The Seven Military Classics of Ancient China," Westview Press Inc, Boulder, Colorado, USA, 1993.

Robert D Fisher Jr, "China's Military Modernization", Pentagon Press, New Delhi, 2008.

Scobell, David Lai and Roy Kamphausen (Ed), "Chinese Lessons from Other Peoples War," Lancer Publishers and Distributors, New Delhi, 2012.

Wang Houqing, "The Chinese Army Today, Traditions and Transformations for the 21st century," NDU Press, Beijing, 2000.

William Antholis, "Inside Out India and China", The Brookings Institution, 1775 Massachusetts Avenue, N.W., Washington D.C. 20036, 2013.

Xiaobing Li, "China at War An Encyclopedia", Pentagon Press, New Delhi-110049, 2012.

*

Index